CW01496142

ZIGLAR LE

To my friends
& Elliot
Olya
my best wishes

Zigar
April 2016

ZIGLAR
LEGACY

**Inspiring Stories from
Ziglar Legacy Certified Trainers**

Copyright© 2014
Michelle Prince
Performance Publishing Group
McKinney, Texas

All Worldwide Rights Reserved, McKinney, Texas

All rights reserved. No part of this publication may be reproduced, stored in a retrieval system, or transmitted, in any form, or by any means, electronic, mechanical, recorded, photocopied, or otherwise, without the prior written permission of the copyright owner, except by a reviewer who may quote brief passages in a review.

ISBN 13: 978-0-9906553-1-2

FOREWORD

I HAVE A question for you. Are you the pinball in the game of life, getting bounced around by circumstances beyond your control, or are you on a mission driven by a purpose and fueled by passion? Or maybe you have big dreams but life seems to get in the way, and your dreams get dimmer and dimmer as the days go by. Good news! It doesn't matter if you are on the fast track to your dreams or if you are lost in a nightmare, this book will give you the inspiration and courage you need to be, do, and have all that life has to offer.

My father always loved stories of hope and inspiration from real people who overcame great circumstances to make a positive difference in the world. Why? Because he understood that all of us are unique and each of us will respond differently when we read about the successes of others. It all boils down to this simple idea: "If he can, if she can, I can." That, in a nutshell, is why I love this book and believe it will have an incredible impact in your life.

One more thing. This book is different in another big way. When one of these stories inspires you or challenges you, I encourage you to reach out and speak with the author personally. The message of this book is not complete without you being changed for the better in some way. Every author in this book is dedicated to helping you become the person God created you to be. And this, above everything else, is why I know my dad is proud to have these men and women carrying on the Ziglar Legacy.

Tom Ziglar
CEO-Proud Son of Zig Ziglar

TABLE OF CONTENTS

Little Giants and the Doormat

Dr. Diyari Abdah... 1

Adoption, A Starfish and Zig

Tracy D. Day... 11

The Power of Choice

Mahongo Fumbelo 21

Learning to Believe in His Plan

Ken Grant.. 39

Connect the Dots

Nikki Ivey.. 51

How Seven Steps to Goal Setting Helped Save My Life

Karl Kispert 65

Exponential Impact

James McLamb 81

Lessons Through Adversity

David Mineer.. 91

It's Only Hard 'Til You Learn It

Michael Ray Newman... 103

Time for Change

Rick Richards 115

The Excellence Effect

Justin Young 137

LITTLE GIANTS AND THE DOORMAT

By Dr. Diyari Abdah

IT WAS A beautiful sunny morning in Plano, Texas, and students ("Little Giants") were arriving from six different countries and five continents for a life-changing transformational journey at the Ziglar headquarters.

Personally, entering the building and walking through the place where my mentor, the legendary Mr. Zig Ziglar, was once teaching his wisdom, was as grand as entering Plato's Academy in Athens in 399 B.C. There was this extraordinary feeling that you could almost feel Zig's presence, and his charismatic voice was in my ear most of the time.

Zig Ziglar established his own voice in modern philosophy, and you can't help but remember and live by his quotes, which millions of people every day and everywhere share and repeat in conversations, talks, and speeches, and on social media around the globe.

During trips to places of significance, you always find people sitting in a corner or on a rock almost in a meditative state, absorbing the significance of the place and trying to imagine what was it like when those people of significance were in action, and wondering how their world felt on a daily basis. The same happened to others as happened to me when we visited Ziglar Inc., HQ. We were wondering what it was like to be Zig Ziglar, one of the most influential speakers of his generation. He must have come out of that door and gone into the other with some papers in his hand, preparing for his next talks and teaching opportunities. Perhaps he liked to joke with one of his lucky staff who was with him, and so on.

To be surrounded by his beloved family, during the five days of training on the Ziglar Legacy Certification Course, for any devoted Ziglar fan, is something that you cannot put a price on. They shared their stories of "home and daily life with Zig Ziglar" with us, and, as Zig himself was a "master storyteller," he would have given each one them a ten out of ten for their story-telling skills. Purely and simply AWESOME! Sometimes the stories made us cry. And sometimes we were almost falling on the ground laughing. It showed what kind of a MAN he was. A man who valued life and lived by example and principles, but at the same time was full of joy and laughter and passion for helping others and enhancing their lives.

Many people say, "I want to be the next Zig Ziglar," which I am sure for the family and the fans is a huge compliment, but even his own proud son, and my brother, Mr. Tom Ziglar, CEO of Ziglar Inc., says himself that he is NOT Zig Ziglar, nor does he want to be. There is only one Plato, one Picasso, one Mozart, one Gandhi—and one Zig Ziglar. People can learn from his teachings and wisdom and teach others and live by his example, but NO ONE can be Zig Ziglar. He came from a certain background, certain parents, a certain town—Yazoo City, Mississippi. And he went through certain events in life that made him who he was. Therefore, it is impossible to become the next Zig Ziglar. However, with enough passion for helping others unconditionally, and enough enthusiasm and discipline, one has the potential of creating his own legacy and being compared to and among great people, just like Mr. Ziglar did.

On the first day, the "Little Giants" were sitting in class, excited about what was coming next—and I say "Little Giants" with greatest respect for all my classmates, because they were truly giants in what they were already doing or setting themselves up to do. Some were already running very successful companies, and others had to sell possessions to get there and start their journey to change people's lives in the future. The individual stories were so powerful that they could have been taught in a separate course as lessons in life.

These were not ordinary people; they were giants who were destined to do bigger and greater things in life through their own experiences and the teachings of their mentors and particularly Mr. Zig Ziglar, who lives with us now every single day. WOW, talk about legacy and immortality! I don't think it can get any bigger than this in MY lifetime.

We were all very excited and looking forward to the week ahead, and not knowing exactly what to expect. And, now the BIG question on my mind was if virtue could be taught.

As a dental surgeon and a student of life, I am always advancing my knowledge and on the lookout for new ideas and teachings that fill my knowledge gaps. Because Anything Worth Doing Is Worth Doing Better—and that's how I started my journey over ten years ago with Mr. Ziglar. But there was also another element in the mix: frustration.

My personal journey started out of frustration. I was looking for answers on how to communicate effectively with others, especially my patients, in order to create a more positive environment for everyone. After all, going to the dentist is not on people's list when it comes to "The Ten Most Recreational and Relaxing Ways to Spend Your Day."

Communicating effectively with patients and having a heart-to-heart discussion is vital for everybody, but not easy—especially when you are talking to someone who is so nervous that they only remember 20 percent of the conversation. We've all been there, I am sure. Its important that people (clients/patients) are feeling relaxed, so that way they can see the value in what is being presented to them. It is especially important for us in the healthcare business. We know that we have a very important message to get across and we must make sure that the patient knows and realizes that we are all on the same team and working together to improve something they want. We cannot be creating that glass wall that you experience in most discussions and during consultations with some professionals.

I started listening to all the Zig Ziglar audio tapes—Yes, tapes!—that I could put my hands on. There was a lot of wisdom in every sentence, but I was looking for that magic phrase to use on Monday morning when I was back in the office that could make all the difference. I thought there was some magic formula for this, or that there were certain phrases that only Mr. Ziglar could teach through his audio seminars and teachings. After all he was labeled "the man who could sell anything to anyone!" And by "selling" here I mean selling an idea, or an opinion, or your point of view or suggestion, and not necessarily a physical sale.

Very quickly, like most Ziglar fans, I got hooked on the stories he was telling with his captivating voice and it became a routine to listen to "Uncle" Zig every night before going to sleep. So many times I have woken up in the morning with headphones still attached to my ears. This is something we hear often from Ziglar fans. As if that wasn't enough, in the "automobile university," again it had to be Ziglar's mesmerizing voice and not the news. After all, it was much better to listen to Zig Ziglar than the news—and even today that is still the case.

Hearing the stories over and over, and listening to his messages and the stories behind the stories, opened a whole new level of understanding to what and why he was sharing his wisdom in that way. In fact, in a very simple yet clever way, he was telling stories about life and drawing lessons from them. We all love stories, and that's why he was telling these stories with his messages and teachings embedded in them, so they would all make sense, instead of offering an impersonal and soulless style of Do and Don't bullet points.

Yes, there is certain methodology in presenting a solution to a client or patient; and Yes, there are certain ways of saying things in the right order; and Yes, the way the information is presented can make all the difference in the client/patient/friend agreeing to what you say. But in the end it all comes down to one simple thing that all human beings can Do and Need, and that is speaking from the heart—being genuine and treating people with dignity and respect no matter what, and then doing even more: going beyond their expectations. Then, and only then, can you expect what you want in return.

> "You can have everything in life you want if you will just help enough other people get what they want." —Zig Ziglar

How powerful and life-changing this statement is! It's one I live by every day now, and it's made a huge difference in my life. It made me love to go to meet my team and friends (patients) and not go to work to see staff and patients. It made me realize that there are many different ways to be helpful to my patients (friends) than just by treating their problems. It made me discover that "I" could achieve more and help more in the process. It made me believe that one day my message could become global; and it made me realize my goal of becoming a best-selling author and being awarded for it in Hollywood, California. It led me to receiving an award as Best Speaker in 2014 in New York City and being interviewed by a three-time Emmy award–winning director and producer. It resulted in me being invited to speak internationally and touch people's lives.

All this because of one simple philosophy that anyone can apply in their life if they want to—and this is not to impress you but simply to remind you that anything is possible when you put your mind to it, when you surround yourself with the people who are willing to add value to your life unconditionally, which is what I have learned to do.

So a big Thank You to all my mentors and friends who believed in me, and especially to my mentor, Mr. Zig Ziglar, through his teachings and sharing his wisdom, which is enriching our lives.

Now, back to the idea of "Little Giants and the Doormat". You may wonder, What is this story of the doormat? As I mentioned, I realized from day one during our training at Ziglar HQ that I was in the presence of giants—my fellow students—and because we were learning new skills I affectionately gave the experience this description: Little Giants in the Ziglar World. On the second morning, a few of us were standing outside, enjoying the sunny morning in Texas, when we happened to notice that in front of the main door there was a doormat with the Ziglar Inc. logo on it which says "ZIGLAR." It is a fairly wide doormat with ZIGLAR beautifully written across it to make a statement as you walk in.

We happened to notice that almost every student tried to avoid stepping on the word ZIGLAR that was designed into the doormat. Then it became an obsession among a few of us. On days three and four we watched to see if that happened again; and we were not surprised to see that, again and again, most people were hopping over the mat entirely to get inside or walking around the letters ZIGLAR. This moved all of us who were observing this, and I even told the CEO and my good friend and brother, Mr. Tom Ziglar, that they might want to change the mat or redesign it, because people are simply refusing to walk on the name.

That is the ultimate sign of respect in my opinion that people can't even step on a doormat because it has the name ZIGLAR on it. And one thing I have learned in my five decades on earth is that: "RESPECT is something you work for very hard on a daily basis, and you earn it. And one day when you do eventually earn it, people will simply refuse to walk on your name out of respect."

Being one of the lucky students accepted into the Ziglar Legacy Certification Training was a life-changing experience. Being part of a select group of giants who want to make this world a better place, regardless of origin and religion, is just priceless. It is very emotional to graduate as a Ziglar Legacy Certified Trainer, and I am honored and humbled to be a Ziglar ambassador for hope in this world. Life is the most precious gift that we have on this earth and, as beautiful as it is, it can have ups and downs.

People sometimes need direction or redirection in life or in business, and as Ziglar Legacy Certified Trainers we are armed with the best tools to help others to find their path and their calling. After all, "From time to time, everybody needs a check-up from the neck up" —Zig Ziglar.

Don't live a mediocre life. You only have one "that you remember."

Be a positive influencer, find strengths in people, and help them find and develop their passion and purpose.

"Don't Be Indifferent. Be a Difference-Maker Instead"
                                        —Diyari Abdah.

Life gives us many opportunities to help others and BE helped. Don't miss out on the opportunities. Maybe it will be YOUR name on that doormat one day that people avoid stepping on. ✑

DR. DIYARI ABDAH

Dr. Diyari Abdah is a best-selling author, award-winning international speaker, cosmetic and implant dental surgeon (he holds two dental degrees and a master of science degree [MSc] in implantology), business developer and coach to dentists, and the first Certified Ziglar Legacy Trainer in the UK. He runs a successful practice in Cambridge, UK. He is CEO of Dental Coaching HQ, where he develops the skills of dentists, doctors, and other professionals on how to effectively improve their business and marketing skills in order to take their businesses to the next level. Through his seminar, "The Art of Reinvention," he presents the road map to positive change by teaching techniques to change people's habits and reinvent themselves. His journey with Ziglar started over ten years ago when he was seeking answers in business and life and managed to find in the Ziglar teachings a model around which to build his success. Over the years, he has become a life-long Ziglar student and now a Certified Ziglar Legacy Trainer. This is reflected in his success after he was certified: his business has tripled in the last five years. Now he wants to share his knowledge with others who are ambitious and aspire to succeed. Dr. Abdah can be reached at:

drabdah@hotmail.com
0044 7971 404098.

ADOPTION, A STARFISH, AND ZIG

By Tracy D. Day

YOU ARE ASKING yourself, "What in the world do those things have in common?" How can adoption, a starfish, and Zig Ziglar all be tied together? The answer is the story of my life and how I became a Ziglar Legacy Certified Trainer.

I was born addicted in the Texas panhandle in the late 1960s. The state immediately put me into foster care. My foster parents made all the difference in my life and put me on this path toward a great life and being a leader. I owe everything I am to Vernon and LaNita Day. They knew from the start that, with the right love and support, I was going to be something special. Three weeks after my birth, mom and dad filed for adoption. My first year in life was tough, but with their love and support things began to come into focus.

Things began to get interesting when I was about 10 years old. My parents told me I was adopted and I started rebelling. I was a bad kid for a few years, but my dad saw more in me than I knew existed. He would always love on me and tell me I was "Born to Win." This was way before Zig wrote his last book, Born to Win. My dad would keep telling me that over and over. Dad would encourage me to be more than I thought was possible, and that it takes effort, focus, and determination. Dad always told me that my reputation would precede me—either good or bad. I had to make a choice how to live my life and be a servant leader.

As we all know as adults, most teenagers don't listen to the wisdom of their parents. We all know that teenagers know everything there is to know in life and how to deal with what falls into their lap. As you chuckle from that last statement, you were thinking "Yup, I knew it all"; or "I wish I had listened to my parents back then." I fall into the latter category. As I began to gain more wisdom and understanding, I turned things around and began to work on who I was becoming as a man.

I was raised in a good home in a small town. Everyone knew each other and whose kids belonged to whose parents. My dad served in the Texas National Guard for 35 years and it seemed as if everyone worked for my dad once a month and two weeks a year. Everyone knew my dad personally or knew who he was. Dad, due to his job as a Command Sergeant Major and First Sergeant, and more so to who he was as a man, was a servant leader. All the parents knew what child belonged to what family and would keep the kids from misbehaving. The adage "it takes a village to raise a child" was true where I lived. The small farming community was a great place to live and grow up during my high school years.

The leadership in me began to blossom during this time in my life. My brothers and I earned our Eagle Scout award in the Boy Scouts. I served on the staff at summer camp for a few years teaching others various merit badges. I even earned the American Red Cross Water Safety Instructor certification my last year on staff. It was a great summer. That fall I was elected by my classmates to be the senior class vice president. Granted, it was high school, but it was a title nonetheless, and I believed that I was beginning to understand what my parents had been telling me all those years. I was a winner, a leader, and I made a difference to those around me. I had the reasonability to help others and be a servant leader. All that I was at that point in my life was due to the love and support of my parents, my brothers, and my extended family. I was born to another, but my adopted family—my family—loved me.

I didn't know it at the time, but the foundation for receiving Zig Ziglar's message and teachings had been laid. Zig said in *See You at the Top* that parents feed children love, obedience, faith, and integrity. The life lessons we learn as children will stick with us as we grow into adulthood.

Everyone has heard the stories of a grandfather and his grandchild walking on the beach talking about various life lessons. One such story includes the grandfather throwing starfish that washed ashore back into the ocean. As they walked, the small boy said, "Grandpa, why are you throwing those things back into the water?"

The grandfather simply and lovingly replied, "These are starfish. These are living things. They belong in the water to live."

As the grandfather reached down and tossed a few more into the ocean, they continued to walk. Every few steps, another starfish or two was tossed back into the ocean.

The young child asked, "Grandpa, why do you keep throwing the starfish back into the ocean? You can't throw them all back. There are millions of them."

I doubt there were millions of them, but to a small child, it must have seemed that way. However, the grandfather knew something the child had not really comprehended in his young life. The grandfather stopped, kneeled down to the child's level, looked him in the eye and said, "Sweetheart, I do what I can to help those around me. It gives me joy to know I make a difference." With that he reached down and picked up another starfish and tossed it back into the ocean.

The young child picked one up as well and threw it as far has he could. He looked at his smiling grandfather and enthusiastically said, "We made a difference to those two, didn't we grandpa?"

"Yes, we did!"

I encourage you to pause for a moment and think about that story. You may have heard it many times before, as I have, or it may be the first time you have heard that story. I ask that you think for a moment what your parents have taught you. I hope they have shared positive lessons with you. I think we all need a word of encouragement in our lives, especially now. Open a door for someone and cheerfully say, "Good Morning." I have seen firsthand how a daily positive attitude will foster a healthy, positive environment at home, at work, and in everything about our daily lives. The exponential growth of doing something positive and uplifting to those around will come back to you. Zig said, "The choice to have a great attitude is something nobody or no circumstance can take away from you." I am a firm believer in that statement. I choose to laugh and have a positive attitude every day. Zig made a difference and had a positive attitude every day. It became contagious to everyone who had an association with Zig.

I was recently at a workshop event in the Dallas, Texas, area, and I was introduced to a friend of Zig Ziglar. During the workshop, I had the opportunity to tell a little bit of my life story to the group. Although I had heard the starfish story hundreds of times, I never really integrated it fully into my own life until that day. Zig's friend stated to me that I was a starfish and that my parents saved me and gave me life—a great life.

His comments hit me hard, like a ton of bricks. I had to take a moment and look within myself with a newfound sense of love and purpose. I literally sat there to process the comment and the moment. I had never looked at my life in that manner. He was right, I was the starfish on the beach at birth. My parents adopted me and this was my version of getting tossed back into the ocean to live again and have a second chance at life.

As an adult, I had made some choices in life that were not the greatest. I wound up working three jobs during my early 20s just to make ends meet and meet my financial obligations. I knew hard work and focus and taking pride in the family name was the only way to go, even though I thought I had tarnished the name due to my lack of good judgment.

I was exposed to some business people during that time, and one of them suggested I read some positive mental attitude or PMA books. Even though I had some great teachings from my parents, I was never exposed to some of those authors in my youth. It was a "who's who" list of great motivators and leaders. Among them was Zig Ziglar's book, *See You at the Top*.

I was done. Who is this guy? Zig would always say, "I was born in L.A., that's Lower Alabama and raised in East Texas, otherwise known as Mississippi." I instantly related to his messages, his delivery, and his voice. Zig had a calming but encouraging tone in his messages whether you were reading or listening to an audio of him speaking. I learned that Zig had this unique ability to encourage, motivate, uplift, and truly inspire his audiences. I could see the bricks in my foundation were exactly like Zig's in that he lived with integrity, loyalty, and high character.

I saw some of my dad in Zig. Yes sir, I liked this guy.

I mentioned earlier that teenagers don't always listen to their parents, but somewhere along the trail of life all teenagers eventually have that "Ah-Ha" moment and realize that what mom and dad had been saying was true. I had my "Ah-Ha" moment, and Zig delivered it right in my face. I knew I had to take action.

I called my parents and said I would be home that weekend. I simply told them I loved them and appreciated all they had done for me in my life. It was a great weekend of really bonding and appreciating each other. It was great to really learn again from them as they continued to tell me stories from my childhood that I had forgotten.

Zig was right on target in his famous quote, "You can have everything you want, if you help enough people get what they want." I was a witness to that every day of my life watching my dad serve others. Dad wanted for nothing. He and mom never argued, were always happy, and simply enjoyed live. He lived that way for the remainder of his life. Regretfully, my dad passed Memorial Day weekend in 2010. Fittingly, he received a full military funeral. The entire community showed great support to my mom and family. I am thankful for the man he was and how much he molded me into the man I am today.

I also served in the military, and I modeled my career after my dad. I was a servant leader and was always helping those around me. I knew I could do more and be more. I began looking and searching for more. If the right opportunity revealed itself, I knew what it would be.

Social media delivered. I saw a post about a webinar hosted by Tom Ziglar, the proud son of Zig Ziglar. I watched the webinar and I knew what I had to do. I spoke with my wife and we made the decision to act! I called and spoke with the staff at Ziglar, Inc. The paperwork and application process was complete and I eagerly waited for that call. It came. I was accepted to be a Ziglar Legacy Certified Trainer.

Tom Ziglar had an initial conference call with all those selected for this class. The very first thing he said was that the Ziglar Family felt like adopting all the class members because we all spoke as if Zig was a second father to all of us. Tom's words hit home with me. I was adopted at birth and given a second chance. This second adoption for me is just as important. However, this provides me an avenue to continue to spread the values and teachings of Zig to others.

The morning of the first day was overwhelming. The room was filled with people I considered successful. Everyone was dressed professionally, carried themselves as professionals, and all were in such a great mood. The energy in the room was off the charts and continued throughout the remainder of the course. The joy of having been touched by Zig Ziglar, just as I had been, was being shared by everyone. Their respective stories of the first time they heard Zig, or read one of his books, or even saw him in person were each as unique as we all were, but the solid common bond was how Zig improved their lives. I never had the luxury of seeing Zig in person, but to have his books and video of him now makes it great to have him with me as I speak his time-tested messages on all things "Ziggy."

The certification class in the Dallas area was simply outstanding. It was my honor to be in the same class with some of the best small-business leaders and motivators. I was deserving to be in the room. It has been and still is an honor to be a fellow classmate with these outstanding men and women.

Wow! What a great ride this has been the last few months as a Zig Ziglar Legacy Certified Trainer. You bought this book because you know and appreciate the Ziglar brand or the principles and foundation upon which Mr. Zig Ziglar built his life. You may be a family member or a friend of one of the coauthors. I am sure you have enjoyed reading all the great stories of the other coauthors and the impact that Zig had on their life. Zig's impact on my life has been phenomenal and is no different from the other legacy trainers or even from you. Live your life to the fullest just as Zig did, and be an encourager to others. Choose to have a positive attitude every day. The blessings will come back to you multiplied.

Zig has hundreds of quotes, each one with its own special meaning to him and to each of us. One special quote to me is something Zig said by which I live my life to this day. Zig said, "Positive thinking won't let you do anything, but it will let you do everything better than negative thinking will."

I challenge you to adopt a positive thinking attitude. I challenge you to go save a "starfish" that needs your help, no matter how small or big your assistance will be. It matters to the starfish. Finally, continue to live your life on the principles Zig lived his life. I am sure life will be grand and the blessings will overflow to you and your family just as they have in mine. ∾

TRACY D. DAY

Tracy D. Day has worked in the information tech-nology profession for over 28 years. As an infant, Tracy was adopted into a military household. Growing up in a military family and experienc-ing leadership throughout his young life, Tracy be-gan his career in the United States Air Force and served nearly 14 years. Currently, he serves as an IT consultant for the United States Air Force.

Tracy is a Wayland Baptist University graduate. He received his bachelor's in Information Systems Management. Tracy holds a variety of technical cer-tifications in the IT field. He also owns a financial services business and is currently licensed at the state and federal levels.

He has been involved in various leadership roles throughout his career. While in the Air Force, Tracy held the role of Local Area Network Manager. As a con-sultant, he was hand-selected to lead a team of individuals for a national project that covered the country coast to coast, including Alaska. He currently serves in a role that works closely with Microsoft and other federal agencies and impacts millions. Tracy has presented and spoken at a number of technical conferences and to senior management in a variety of organizations.

In Tracy's financial services career, he has been called upon to conduct train-ing with small organizations in his local area. Tracy was hand-selected by the Ziglar Corporation to be among the first 40 Ziglar Legacy Certified trainers and speakers in the world. Tracy speaks on building winning relationships, goal setting and achievement, building a better you, and other leadership principles.

Being adopted into a loving family changed his life to the tune of having a good-natured, fun-loving attitude. He demonstrates that same attitude with his wife and three children. Tracy's approach and belief is to have a positive impact on everyone he meets and to make a difference in their life.

Tracy D. Day
tracy@tracydaymotivation.com
www.tracydaymotivation.com

THE POWER OF CHOICE:

By Mahongo Fumbelo

Getting hurt is inevitable; living like a victim is a choice. It takes the same energy to choose healing as it does bitterness—but the results are different. One leaves you paralyzed by the past; the other gives you hope for the future.

—Devotional, United Christian Broadcasters, Australia, 9/19/05

FROM A VERY young age, my parents affirmed to me that they were not going to bring me up as a woman or as an African child but as a human being deserving of every good thing life has to offer. They taught me that success in life was not a matter of your skin color, personal appearance, or sheer luck. Integrity, excellence, kindness, respect for others, love, forgiveness, and hard work featured boldly in every conversation I had with my parents regarding success. They stressed to me that good things really did come to those who hoped, persevered, and worked as hard as they could, even when no one was watching.

As much as my parents loved me and gave me as much positive affirmation as any child could get, they also made me aware of life's challenges and obstacles. I had no idea, however, that my biggest challenge was going to be about coping with the death of my father when he died in 1999. I felt that my father had gone too soon. My career as a journalist was just about to take off. I had looked forward to coming home to tell my father about my biggest stories, and I always anticipated his insightful encouragement and wisdom. My father had always told me that I could be anything I wanted to be in life, and he gave me the freedom to choose. I had never lost someone so close to me before, and the reality of going through my adult life without my biggest fan, my father, was too overwhelming to face.

Although I was a believer, and I knew that even good people did die, I found myself questioning God. "Why my father, God? Why this time? Who is going to read my newspaper stories and give me constructive feedback and encouragement? Who is going to walk me down the aisle? Who will give that wedding speech? Why me, God?"

The hardest part of my grief was to imagine how my mother was going to cope without her soul mate. My mother and my father were inseparable. They made marriage look so desirable. Their love and support for each other was so visible in everything they did. The more I questioned God about my father's untimely death, the more I felt bitter and angry. I was guilty too that as a Christian I failed to understand that death was something we were all bound to go through. I had heard so many sermons about death and how to grieve as a Christian, but I failed to apply the word at my time of grieving. If this was a test, I did everything at the time not to attempt to pass it.

The answers to my questions about why God would let my father die at that time did not come when I was bitter. Rather, they came when I realized that how I was going to respond to my father's death was really going to determine how I would respond to every other tragedy I was going to face in life. I recognized that I had a choice to be sad about my father's death, or to celebrate his life and believe that he was still cheering me on from the balcony of heaven. I had to make that choice in spite of the harsh reality of not having him physically present.

Shortly after my father's death, my boss told me that the United Nations was looking for people to go to East Timor to assist with the referendum. I had never heard of East Timor until then. My daring spirit soon convinced me that this was an adventure worth signing up for. Without any hesitation, I told my boss to put my name down. Soon, word spread about my impending travel to an island that everyone in my country thought was the most dangerous place on earth. My family feared for my life and tried unsuccessfully to talk me out of making the dangerous journey.

Indonesia had occupied East Timor for nearly 24 years. The East Timorese who tried to oppose the regime suffered the worst brutality imaginable. Torture, assassinations, kidnapping, rape, and imprisonment were rife. For me, this was convincing enough that helping the East Timorese decide the political destiny of their tiny island was going to be the best thing I had ever done in my life. With this resolve, I packed everything I could and set off on what I knew was going to be an adventure I would never forget.

The training base for United Nations civilians for the mission in East Timor was Darwin, Northern Territory, Australia. Soon after my training in Darwin, I hopped into the belly of a C130 transport aircraft with other United Nations crew to start our mission. As we landed at the tiny airport in the town of Baucau, it was very clear who was in charge. Indonesian military and police clad in army fatigues and khaki brandishing their military apparatus scrutinized our passports before ushering us into the airport's arrival terminal.

As we were chauffeur-driven from the airport in our brand new Land Rovers with the two letters, UN, boldly plastered on their sides, we were cheered on by hope-filled throngs of East Timorese. Old and young, they had lined both sides of the narrow one-way street to our dilapidated motel. They had waited for the UN to come and rescue them from the misery and brutality of the Indonesian regime. They accorded us the status of heroes who had come to save their lives. My heart was filled with fear of failure to live up to their expectations. As these thoughts were rushing through my mind, the surrounding tin dwellings and the children running around with bare feet soon made me realize the extent of the abject poverty on this beautiful island. I soon appreciated how blessed I was for what I had in my life.

As I got to know the locals more, they began to trust me and confide in me. I met children as young as five who had lost their fathers in the island's quest for freedom. I soon realized that I had had more time with my father than these children did with their fathers. I felt that I was so blessed and that it was up to me to let my father rest in peace. My bitterness and grief about the loss of my father turned into gratitude and beautiful memories. I soon discovered that the reason I went to East Timor was not to help the Timorese but to be reminded of how much I had to be grateful for.

The referendum in East Timor came at a heavy cost for the East Timorese but, in the end, justice won. We did not really manage to stop those who opposed justice and freedom from unleashing more violence when the referendum favored the majority of the Timorese. The Indonesian regime could not leave without a fight, but the Timorese were ready for the sacrifice. The escalation of the violence caused the UN to evacuate all staff to Darwin. The beautiful island of East Timor was burned to the ground. The UN had to establish another mission to help the East Timorese rebuild the island.

Again, I put my hand up to go back to East Timor even though I had only been married for three months. My wonderful husband Mwiya encouraged me to go and do what I loved to do best—help other people. Mwiya later joined me in East Timor and we both worked for the UN until I realized I was pregnant with our first child.

The news about my pregnancy brought so much joy to us. Our joy and hope was tested, however, when I learned one day that I was bleeding heavily and the evidence did not look very good. Mwiya rushed me to the doctor at a local clinic who gave us the news we had dreaded. The news that I was having a miscarriage was devastating for both of us. As we went home to prepare for the next stage of the miscarriage, both Mwiya and I threw ourselves in our bed and sobbed helplessly. All we had longed for was to hold our tiny baby in our hands, and we could not let that dream die.

I still don't have any idea what followed after the sobbing, but somehow in the midst of my despair, I swung into the most faith-filled prayer I had ever prayed. I spoke in tongues for nearly five minutes nonstop. When I finished, I felt as if a ton of bricks had been lifted off my shoulders. Mwiya who had listened to me go into the hullabaloo of tongues, simply muttered, "Honey you are blessed." With that, we both looked at each other and resolved at the same time that we needed to go and take an ultrasound and see another doctor for a second opinion.

The only place we could take the ultrasound at that time was at a Japanese army base. I'm not sure if 3D technology existed then, in 2003, but the ultrasound was so clear that we could see most of the body features of our unborn baby! His posture was as if he was waving at us with his little hand and saying, "I am still here, and I'm okay." We grabbed the results of the scan and went to the nearby hospital. The doctor said she would take another ultrasound and her announcement that the baby seemed to be alive in spite of all the bleeding was the best news any parent to be could ever hope for. Mwiya and I left the hospital almost singing as we praised God for what was one of the greatest miracles we had ever experienced. Although the doctor warned that I couldn't work for a while, that did not matter to us. This also signaled the end of my career with the UN, and I turned down my appointment to go to Kosovo. The doctor also advised that it was probably better for us to go and have our baby in Darwin to ensure I got the best medical care.

On November 12, 2003, Zunga was born. I could not contain the joy of holding this little miracle in my hands. This was the child I was told I was losing through a miscarriage a few months before. I was now holding him in my hands—I could not help but marvel at the miracle. Two and half years later Mwiya and I would welcome our second baby, Wana, born on June 14, 2006. Although I experienced the same miscarriage threats with Wana, I was able to cope better. I knew that my God would see me through again. Wana arrived, healthy and sound—again I counted my blessings.

After two babies, my body had certainly gone through every transformation that any mom can relate to. I weighed nearly 80 kilos (176 pounds). I moved from being a perfect size six to a size 14. I remember trying on one of my favorite outfits, and I could not even manage to pull the pants beyond my hips. My Mwiya was observing me struggle to fit into my pants and he said, "My little Mahongo is gone." He didn't say it in an offensive way, but I vowed to swing into action. I went to a lawn sale at a local school and bought two pieces of exercise equipment for $11.00. It was the best money I ever spent on weight-loss gear.

There were many times when it was tough to balance motherhood and exercise, but it was worth it. My sister had sent me a quote, originally by Joe Sabah and then emphasized by Zig Ziglar. The quote, "You don't have to be great to start, but you have to start to be great," was plastered on a picture of an overweight woman looking at those words. I hopped on the two exercise machines whether I had had little sleep or I wasn't feeling great. Sometimes my joy only came after I had exercised, even though the start was difficult. I exercised three times a day, and within four months I was back to my pre-baby weight, 53 kilos (117 pounds), and a perfect size 6!

While nursing my two boys in Darwin, East Timor was grabbing world news headlines again. The island was in flames again. Riots and violence overshadowed the fragile democracy. Mwiya phoned me to tell me that it was not safe to take our two boys to East Timor. We had to extend our stay in Darwin until further notice.

When Wana was six months old, a lady by the name of Frederica Gaskell called me and asked me to facilitate a workshop for about 27 youths, mostly migrants. Frederica had met me in a shopping mall three months earlier and given me her business card; she told me to call her if I ever needed help with anything. I had so much respect for her from that day. When she asked me to facilitate the workshop, I obliged, although I was not really sure if I could pull it together. Frederica had so much confidence in me, and her support convinced me that I could do it.

As I had no work visa at the time, I could not be paid for facilitating the workshop, but I was more than thrilled to go pro bono. Most of the participants in the workshop were refugees who had fled war in their countries. Some of them were born in refugee camps. I felt honored to have the opportunity to help them restore their hope and be the winners they were born to be.

With a six-month-old baby and a toddler, preparing for the workshop proved to be a challenge. I asked a friend to babysit my boys while I facilitated the workshop. I could hear my baby Wana crying from the other end of the building as I delivered a session. At one point, Zunga, who was nearly three, sneaked away from the babysitter and came and held me by my skirt as I spoke in front of the participants. I was certainly experiencing the joys of motherhood and work.

I wondered what the participants and Frederica who had hired me to facilitate the workshop thought of me and my skills. I was however humbled to hear all the positive feedback the participants had given. A few weeks later, I received another call from Frederica saying they were looking for someone to fill a position in the company she worked for, and she thought I was the best candidate to fill the role. We later discovered that, again, my visa status would make it difficult for me to apply for the job.

Frederica would not easily give up on me. A couple of days before my visa in Australia expired, she called me again saying there was a training organization looking for a lecturer and someone who could coordinate a refugee project for them. I didn't really feel that I had what it took to apply for the job but, out of respect for Mama Frederica, I agreed to attend the job interview. I had only had three hours of sleep the previous night. I didn't think I had answered any of the questions intelligently during that interview. I spoke very casually and I remember cracking a joke during the interview and my two interviewers seemed amused. They called me later and told me that I was hired, and that they would start the skilled migrant visa sponsorship process. I set off to my country Zambia to await the stamp in my passport before returning to Australia.

After nearly 12 months my visa was granted and again, I hopped onto the plane with my boys. As Mwiya was still working in East Timor, I lived as a single married woman in Darwin. We had to make the sacrifice as we wanted to ensure that Mwiya had a job in Darwin before he quit his job in East Timor.

One of my conditions for my new job was to complete two qualifications to gain the competence for the role. My visa dictated that I had to work full-time, 38 hours a week. I had Zunga in preschool and Wana in childcare. I had to pick up Zunga from preschool during my lunch times and rush him to the childcare center and then pick them both up after I finished work. Three hours of sleep each night was the best luxury I could afford. Trying to juggle work, motherhood, and school was almost impossible. My boss at the time would constantly ask how far I had gone with completing my certification for me to keep my job. I said to him that I was doing my best but I could clearly see he was running out of patience.

One day, my boss confronted me in a way I thought was very unnecessary. He gave me an ultimatum to complete the qualification or he was going to take further action. I didn't feel at the time that he understood my circumstances. While I understood that I needed to complete the qualification for compliance, I just felt that I did not deserve to be treated in the manner I was.

I struggled to wake up each day to go to a job where I felt humiliated and unappreciated. Mr. Zig Ziglar's words about maintaining a positive attitude in spite of your circumstances did not make sense to me at the time. Every time I felt discouraged I could almost hear Mr. Ziglar's words echoing in my ears, "Getting knocked down in life is a given. Getting up and moving forward is a choice. Your attitude is your choice, not a result of your circumstances."

Not only had I listened to Mr. Ziglar's tapes, I eventually started to live by the philosophies he talked about. It was hard to maintain a positive attitude in the negative environment in which I found myself. But the more I listened to Mr. Ziglar's messages about keeping a good attitude, the more I thought I could do it. And when I felt I had done my part and gone as far as I could, I felt as though Mr. Ziglar was telling me, "Go one more step farther, Mahongo." Again, it was painful and yet so fulfilling, particularly when I did things right even though no one was watching.

I eventually completed my studies within the time frame I was given. The experience had left me physically drained but still hopeful that my best days were ahead of me. After 18 months, I left the company to get a job with another company.

Six months after joining the new company, I was asked if I was interested in coordinating an employment-focused project for refugees and migrants. Although this was only a temporary assignment and I was told I would return to my original role once the project was finished, I embraced the new role with vigor. I loved every aspect of my job. I have always had a great passion for refugees. I felt that I was born to bring hope and love to people who had experienced some of the worst atrocities and injustice inconceivable to humankind.

One of my clients who had lived in a refugee camp for 13 years told me that she thought she had a better war in her country than the war her husband had in his country. I wondered what made one war better than the other, and I asked her to elaborate. She said, "Well, at least the militia didn't kill my entire family during the war in my country. My husband lost his entire family in the war in his country, and he was only 12 years old when it happened." This woman went on to tell me how she had met her husband in a refugee camp before coming to Australia as refugees. Her resilience and perseverance were a living personification of Ziglar's philosophy that indeed what matters is how you respond to the circumstances, not what happens to you. I couldn't have been more convinced that the best I could do was to go the extra mile in helping people who had already endured so much pain and injustice.

One of my most joyful times in my job was to put refugees into jobs, particularly when they had experienced so much rejection from countless job applications. I was privileged to have the opportunity to lobby employers to give refugees a go at employment, and in most cases they didn't disappoint. The results from the refugee project were overwhelming. More than 50 percent got employment or training out of it. A number of the participants also completed their qualification in a trade or related area in spite of their low English language proficiency. It was the first qualification for most of them as they didn't have a chance to go to school in their country. I saw refugees, who were told repeatedly by driving instructors that they were too dumb to learn to drive a car, get their first license. Their success became my success, not because I had made them achieve what they wanted, but because I saw them defy the notion that your circumstances can stop you from becoming your best.

I was humbled when the company gave me an award for placing a significant number of clients into jobs and helping to mentor them to retain their employment for six months and beyond. At the end of the project, my company allowed me to stay in the company and offered me my original position back. This meant that my salary went down by nearly $21,000 per year. I had enjoyed every moment of my role as coordinator of the project. I felt that the experience I had gained in that job was something I would never forget. I resolved to stay with the company in spite of the drop in my pay. I was the longest-serving staff member in the company's regional office after nearly three and a half years.

Soon after the completion of my project, I discovered that I had contracted an airborne disease from a previous client. I was devastated by the news. I wondered whether I would be able to live through the period of the medication. I struggled to have enough energy to do even some of the simplest tasks at home, such as vacuuming or laundry. Driving a car to work became a mission each day. I persevered, however, and put in my best at work.

One day, I turned up at the office, pumped after listening to Mr. Ziglar's message about having a good attitude and getting along with work colleagues even if they rubbed you round the wrong way. As I got to the office, one of my colleagues told me that my boss had asked her if I was in the office and that she had referred to me as a f****** b****. "Mahongo, you need to do something about this," she said. "I think it's wrong for this person to refer to you in such derogatory terms." For a moment, anger swelled up in me. At that time, I believed I was one of the best-performing employees in the office. I had created a lot of good outcomes for the company. I had gone the extra mile. I had worked so hard even when I was struggling with my health. My clients had always wondered why I seemed to do extra for them even when they thought they didn't deserve it. One of my clients had once confided, "Mahongo, no one has ever told me that I could be someone someday, and yet you seem to believe in me, and you go out of your way to make that happen."

I reluctantly put in a complaint about the way I had been treated by my boss. The response I got left me stunned and made me regret having reported the incident in the first place. The senior manager who was asked to preside over the matter resolved that my boss would be given a tin, and she would have to put 50 cents in that tin each time she used a swear word. I felt that my complaint was reduced to mockery. I had read and believed every word about the company values, and none of those values had been reflected in the verdict over my complaint. Again, I could almost hear Mr. Ziglar's words echoing through my ears, "Getting knocked down in life is a given. Getting up and moving forward is a choice. Your attitude is your choice, not a result of your circumstances." I questioned Mr. Ziglar's philosophy. "I have done my part, Mr. Ziglar, surely the other people have to do their part." I struggled to keep a positive attitude, and yet the conviction that it was up to me to get over the situation became stronger each day as I faced those who had humiliated me.

As if what I had experienced was not enough, the same manager who had earlier belittled my complaint came to me and said he didn't think any of my colleagues liked me in the office. He said I had to take a public relations walk around the office and find out how my colleagues felt about me. Again, I wondered how much longer I had to endure this unnecessary mind game. When I had the opportunity, I asked my colleagues why they had gone to the manager and made all the unwarranted allegations about me. None of them would admit it. They said, "In fact, it was the senior manager who talked about you, Mahongo." They told me about how I was talked about during an office dinner which I did not attend due to family commitments.

I knew that it was the least productive use of my energies trying to find out who liked me or who didn't in the office. I retreated to what I usually do in such a situation: I evaluated myself. I asked myself how I was communicating with others, if I was doing my best to be part of the team. I resolved that if I needed to work on a few things I would. Again, I put my Ziglar philosophy into play.

In early 2014, I came across a Ziglar post on Facebook calling on trainers and speakers who wanted to be certified Ziglar Legacy Trainers. I thought that post was specifically sent to me and I literally personal-ized it: "Mahongo, are you a speaker, trainer, consultant, or coach? If you desire to make a positive difference in the world by helping others Be, Do, and Have more, then you need to learn more about the Ziglar Legacy Class." I had no idea how I was going to afford the investment, and yet I was convinced this was something I had to do. I confided in my husband, who not only is my emotional scaffold but my number one fan when it comes to my career. Without any hesitation, Mwiya said, "Babe, this is meant for you, and you'll regret it if you don't go."

Two weeks prior to my departure to Dallas, Texas, for my Ziglar Leg-acy Certification Course, my boss asked me if I wanted to consider taking up an additional role. She told me that she thought I had all the skills, attributes, and qualifications for the role, and she wanted me to consider taking the offer. I agreed.

I was told, however, that I was going to have a meeting with our head office to discuss the role and preparation for it. I was not aware that the meeting was going to be attended by the senior manager who had pre-viously belittled my complaint about how my manager was swearing at me and his allegations that nobody really liked me in the office. During our meeting, he simply retorted, "Mahongo, I don't think you have the right personality for this job." I tried to compose myself as I struggled to understand the meaning behind his comments. I had never felt so humiliated in my entire corporate life. I felt that it would have been easier if this man had simply taken a shot gun and put a bullet through my heart. However, I carried on with the meeting to the end. I thanked everyone for their time and walked back to my desk in a daze.

I struggled to find my energy and productivity. My computer screen looked blurred, not because it was but because I couldn't focus. After five years of serving the company I loved so much, I questioned how much longer I could stand being humiliated for things I had not done.

I composed myself, and I confided in one of my colleagues who had always told me I was a good person to work with. As I told her about my experience, she got teary. She said, "Mahongo, you are too smart to waste your talent for an organization that doesn't appreciate you. I know you can do better in another company. You don't deserve this." My manager also sympathized with me and said she was astonished by the outcome of that meeting. She encouraged me to still think about taking up the role, but I declined.

As I drove home from work that day, I recounted all the humiliation I had endured in the company. I could almost hear the words being said again to me, "Mahongo, nobody likes you in this office, do some public relations and see what your colleagues think of you. Mahongo you're a f****** B****. You don't have the personality for this job. The black one." Their opinions hurt, but they did not change the opinion I had of myself or the opinion people who really knew me had of me. Above all, I knew that God had the best opinion about me. If anything, the negative opinions that this man had about me didn't break me—they made me.

I concluded that again Mr. Ziglar was right, "The only taste of success some people get is when they take a bite out of you." I chose to be the tall poppy that refused to be lopped. I had done my best in my job. I had served the company in the best way I could and, if I had made any mistakes, I had taken the lessons, and it was up to me to use that experience to be the best person I was created to be.

As I contemplated my future, my thoughts were overtaken by one of my favorite Zig Ziglar quotes. And again, I personalized the quote: "Mahongo, you were designed for accomplishment, engineered for success, endowed with the seeds of greatness. Mahongo, you were born to win!"

If there was one more reason why I had to get the Ziglar Legacy Certification, it was my negative experience at work. I felt that the reason I had gone through this humiliating experience at work was so that I could bring hope to other people who might be going through the experience of being put down.

During my graduation speech at the end of the Ziglar Legacy Certification, I had prepared a good and brief story to tell. However, I found myself sharing my story about the humiliation I had endured in my office. I did not plan on making myself so vulnerable and yet the supportive atmosphere at the Ziglar graduation made me feel that it was okay to be vulnerable, and that I could tell the Ziglars almost anything. I couldn't stop myself from crying. I thought I had done the most stupid thing to bring myself to tears. I was shocked when Tom Ziglar, CEO at Ziglar Inc., responded to my speech by saying that he wanted to come to Australia to share the stage with me! He brought out the best in me even when I thought I looked like a mess after all the crying during my speech.

The world seems to be breeding too many experts who have become good at telling people what they can't do. This world needs more people who can become experts at telling people what they are good at, and I want to be that expert at bringing out the good in people.

I want to bring about the good in as many people as I can. There is truly no experience that is bad. It's what we choose to do with the experience that determines the nature of the experience. There is nothing I could do to stop people from humiliating me or attacking me in a negative way, but there is everything I can do to determine to get over it and move forward. The freedom to choose how we respond to our circumstances is a right and a freedom that nobody can take away from us. The Ziglar Legacy Certification has become my license to share my story and help tell other people that, no matter what they have been told or how they feel, they were born to win! ∽

MAHONGO FUMBELO

Mahongo Fumbelo is a trainer, speaker, and employment consultant. She believes that every person in this world has the potential to be the best person they were born to be. Mahongo says she's one of the agents commissioned with the task of helping others unleash their potential in spite of their past negative experiences.

Mahongo's earlier career as a journalist/ public relations consultant and her love for human rights work, took her to East Timor where she worked for the United Nations as an Electoral Officer and later as a Public Information Officer. She co-authored a book on the United Nations staff experiences in East Timor, titled, Viva Timor Leste.

Mahongo has received several awards, including The Elie Wiesel Ethics Award in recognition of her display of dedication to the ideals of international civil service in the UN Mission in East Timor. In 2011, she received the Leading Job Seeker Outcome Award at WISE Employment for her work in placing mostly highly disadvantaged job seekers into employment. She has also won awards for her public speaking, including the Darwin Toast Masters Humorous speech competition. Mahongo also speaks at her local church, C3 Darwin in the Northern Territory, Australia.

Mahongo recently became a Certified Zig Ziglar Trainer, and she says the Ziglar Legacy Certification was the best investment she ever made. She says that her experience during the course has not only changed her thinking and determination to win in life but it has also positively influenced her entire family. Mahongo has now started her own speaking and training business to inspire others to win.

Mahongo lives in Darwin, Northern Territory, Down Under. She has been married to her husband and childhood friend, Mwiya Siakalima, for 14 years, and they have two gorgeous boys, Zunga and Wana.

BornToWinConsulting.com
Twitter @mahongofs
www.ZiglarCertified.com/MahongoFumbelo

LEARNING TO BELIEVE IN HIS PLAN

By Ken Grant

It's not what happens to you that matters. It's how you respond to what happens to you that makes a difference.

—Zig Ziglar

JANUARY 1, 2002. I got up on this wonderful morning looking forward to a new year. I asked the mother of our two boys, then ages seven and four, what her thoughts were for our family goals this year. She floored me with her answer: She wanted a divorce.

When I had finally asked her to marry me just under 10 years before, I had the notion that it would be forever—and I was good with that. I thought that we were making our dreams come true together. Sure, there were ups and downs, and some hard times, but wasn't that what a marriage was? Zig Ziglar has said that more marriages would succeed if the couple would just realize that they are on the same team. I just found out that my teammate wanted to be traded to another team.

I was devastated and didn't know what to think or do. I came up with the idea that I could change her mind. I resolved to be the best husband and father she could ever imagine. You see, up until that fateful day, I thought that the purpose of a husband was to be the provider. I made a good income; I had just had the best year of my life in that respect. For the first time ever I had actually won President's Club, an honor reserved for the very best on the sales force. I thought I had been a good husband, as I did the majority of the cooking and housekeeping. Was giving up my family worth being the best at work? What I thought I could improve on was being more romantic and spending more time with the children. I learned a lot in the next couple of months.

First, I found out that I really didn't know my children. At this point, I didn't even know what size clothes they wore. I beat myself up on that one. Afterwards, I got down to business and found out. I learned who their friends were, and I read to them frequently. We watched shows and movies together. We took walks and went snow skiing. These were things that I never did before because I mistakenly thought I was too busy providing an income.

For my spouse, I tried to do little things that I thought she would like. I doubled my efforts at keeping the household clean and quiet for her. I thought of music that she would like, obtained it, and played it for her. I sat with her and we talked; and I listened, instead of trying to solve the issue and move on. I thought I was doing well, until one afternoon she informed me that there was someone else. Have I already mentioned that I was devastated? Earlier in our marriage, there was a similar incident, and she had promised it would never happen again. I believed her. Now, with this confession, I realized that our marriage would not survive going through this again. I agreed to the divorce and moved into an apartment.

I was very fortunate to be working for the company that I worked for. My direct report was understanding of my situation and let me take the time I needed to get myself back together. My teammates, Mark and Kevin, helped pick up the slack when I couldn't control my emotions on the phone with clients. Donna, Robin, and Nancy would call me daily just to "see how I was doing." This support group was invaluable to me in the coming months. I remember thinking that if I had been with a previous employer, on top of going through a divorce, I would have been unemployed. I remember telling my teammates that "they would have to fire me, because I could never leave a company that supported their people the way they supported me during that period of my life."

I've heard that everything happens for a reason and that we may not know God's plan for us, but to trust in that plan. I learned in the coming months that my plan certainly did not coincide with God's plan. I felt my life was ruined and I found it hard to talk to anyone about it. In my work, although I thought I was successful, I had never shared my personal life with my customers, clients, or workmates. That was about to change.

I was calling on one of our customers, Cindy, and she changed my life. While in her office talking about business, she stopped my presentation and said, "Ken, what's wrong? You don't seem like yourself today." After thirty minutes of being a blubbering idiot, she had my story. I had never in my professional career shared that part of my life. To my surprise, she got up from her desk and walked around to give me a hug—another first for me. Cindy was a wonderful person who personally touched everyone's life that way. She genuinely cared for everyone she met. She is with God now after a battle with cancer. At her memo-rial service, I remember the pastor mentioning that she would pull him aside before the day's service and say, "Now preach good, Pastor, so we can all get His message in our hearts."

She changed my life that day by allowing me to realize that by allow-ing her and her team to see my heart and by caring about what was hap-pening in the personal lives of everyone, everything is better. I changed the way I conducted myself in my business that day. Soon thereafter, I was asked to take a new account manager on the road with me for one week and show him how I conducted business. This was an honor, as I didn't realize I was someone my manager thought of in that way. Sure, I was a top producer, but to train the new guy, Jon, was another matter.

After seeing several accounts on the first day out, Jon was astonished that in every account we visited that day, we received hugs when we got there and as we left. Before retiring for the evening, he said "There is no way every account is like the ones we saw today." I just smiled. The next day we were heading to Cindy's Credit Union and boy, did the love flow there. I don't know if Jon conducts business the way I do, but I do know he shares his thoughts and feelings with his customers the way we did that week.

Now that the divorce was final, I learned that I liked the person I had started to become when I wanted to "save" the marriage. Over the next few years, I read more books on becoming a better person and a loving father to my sons. I wanted to be a good example to them. I felt my obligation to my sons was to make sure they grew up to be young men I would be proud to have my daughter date—if I had a daughter. (I do now have a wonderful stepdaughter, but I didn't know that would happen at the time). Zig said that the "Redhead" (that's how he referred to his wife) is probably the best door opener in all of Dallas; in fact, he said she was written up in the Dallas newspaper, which proclaimed this fact. This was true. As Zig has said, she hadn't opened a door more than five or six times in the sixty-some years they had been married.

That is the type of chivalry I wanted my sons to have. I knew I could not tell them to do this without first being a good example. I looked for ways to show them gentlemanly behavior. I held doors for strangers and made sure I had a smile for everyone, especially for people who didn't have one of their own. One time, when we saw a stranger with their car broken down in the road, we stopped and helped push the car to a safe spot; and then we made sure they had what they needed to get help.

One winter in Colorado, right before Christmas, we got heaps of snow (three to four feet). This is rather unusual in the metropolitan area of Denver. Cars would get stuck driving up the neighborhood street, and when my boys or I saw them, we would quickly get our gear on and go help them dig out, always with three or four other neighbors. And these were not necessarily people we knew. We shoveled each other's sidewalks and made sure (along with several neighbors) that at a couple of houses where some elderly families lived their driveways were shoveled and their mail was retrieved.

During this time, my older son told me that his mother told him there was no Santa Claus. I just looked at him and said "Look around, son; in these last few weeks I've seen lots of them. In the way that everyone helped each other, Santa Claus lives in all of us, son." I was trying to instill that sense of charity and helpfulness in both of my boys, being kind and helpful to everyone. I saw a quote just today, "Being male is a matter of birth. Being a man is a matter of age. But being a gentleman is a matter of choice."

Soon after this time, I thought that it might be nice to try a relationship with another person again. I was scared the same thing would happen as in my failed marriage, so I was determined to make sure it didn't. I had read that if you wanted to change where you were at, you had to change what you were doing. I needed to find a different type of person than my former spouse. I started by sitting down and determining what qualities I wanted in that person. It may seem shallow, but I put down all the qualities I would generally like to have in a woman: pretty, blonde, intelligent, easy to talk too, shorter than me, (I'm not very tall) and several others.

Soon I met Laura; but the relationship almost didn't happen. We met through an online service; and for our first meeting, we were going to have coffee at a coffee shop. I tell you, I almost turned around and missed that meeting. What a mistake that would have been. Laura is an aerospace engineer (a great feat in a world dominated by men). There were only two females in her whole graduating class. Boy, was I in over my head. She is smart, to say the least, and very beautiful. I try to tell her this as much as possible.

I am sitting with her at the coffee shop and mentally going through the list I had made earlier. She had everything—well, almost (she was a redhead). I didn't let that stop me. We made another date, and then another. Soon I knew that I had met the one! We were married 17 months later. By the way, I found out later, that she was a "decided" redhead. By that I mean she had "decided" she was going to be a redhead and became one.

When we were married, she had let her natural color come back. She was a blonde—my list was complete! I still proclaim that I didn't know a marriage could be like this. She is as different in our relationship as the mother of my children as night and day. I'm still not the perfect husband, although I'm better than I was, but Laura handles those imperfections so much differently. She brings up "issues" first from a position of love and trust. That makes all the difference in the world in how I feel and respond.

Laura tells me how she feels, and then it becomes my choice on how I handle it. Of course, I want to make her as happy as she makes me, and that is the path I try to take every day. Laura and I grew up in Aurora, Colorado, about five miles from each other. We went to rival high schools and later to rival in-state universities. When we met, we lived less than six miles apart. It took me 45 years and the trials and tribulations I had gone through to finally be the man who was worthy of her love. Earlier, I talked about God's plan; and now I know what He had in mind—and it is so much more than I ever would have imagined in 2002.

I felt all was right in our world. Laura was wonderful, home life was rolling along, and my job was going well. Little did I know, there was another shake-up about to happen. After having another wonderful year in my job, things were changing. The company had a change in priorities, and everyone from the CEO down to my direct report was replaced—all in less than a year. The saying at work was, "If you just keep your head down and avoid the bullets...." On January 31, 2012, just before my 50th birthday, I was laid off due to this change in company focus. I was shell-shocked. What was I going to do now? I went to tell Laura that I was no longer employed, Laura's response was, "I'm sure that based on your reputation something will come along soon enough and we will be fine. I love you."

I was so very grateful for that response. It was time to work full-time at finding new employment. I didn't realize that in the last 10 years since the divorce what I had learned about sharing my feelings and being a caring person to my accounts would pay off in huge dividends. In 45 minutes after the announcement that I had been laid off, I received my first call. "We heard you are no longer with your previous employer and we would like to talk to you." WOW, someone calling me! I was floored. An hour later, another call came in, then another and another.

I was laid off on a Tuesday, and by Friday I had already completed seven phone interviews. I started interviewing potential companies to see if they would be a good fit for me. Several calls didn't last more than a couple of minutes because I felt they weren't a good fit. I actually suggested some other people who I felt were better fits. It came down to two companies; I traveled to meet them and see their operations. They would both be a good fits for me, and I felt I could contribute to them.

I remember coming home after the second visit and thinking it could be difficult to choose, and I needed to make the right choice. I made the old Ben Franklin list, where you put down all the positives and all the negatives for each company. Once I was done with that, I knew where I would be able to serve the best. After 14 years at my previous employer and having great leadership during my most turbulent times, I never would have imagined the level of the company I chose. This company has been everything I could have asked for, and so much more. My leaders appreciate what I do and listen to my ideas on how to grow. Laura says that my stress level is down tremendously and my relationship with my younger son has grown by leaps and bounds. Again, God's plan had so much more for me than I would have ever imagined or asked for.

In early 2014, I saw an opportunity to become a Ziglar Legacy Certified Trainer. "What an opportunity," I thought—the opportunity of a lifetime. You see, my father took me to see Zig Ziglar speak when I was just 12 years old. He signed his book to me, "See You at the Top!" I read it again and again. I played my father's tapes. I started reading the works of other motivational authors, but I believe it was Zig who guided me to set the goal that eventually helped me make the grades necessary to graduate high school with honors and to go to college.

Laura was supportive of me becoming Ziglar Legacy Certified, and my company was also so very supportive, believing in the benefits. Their support of something I had thought of as a dream meant so very much. I remember the last day of the class, an alumnus of the first ZLC class was there. His comment about feeling "so emotionally charged while feeling so emotionally drained" touched the entire class. We were at Ziglar Headquarters for a week. We laughed, we cried, we hugged, we shared, we felt the presence of Zig Ziglar himself. I remember telling Julie Ziglar Norman about how I had told Laura that this was the opportunity of a lifetime when I told her I wanted to be part of this. After this week at Ziglar, meeting Tom, Julie, and yes, the Redhead, it was so much more than the opportunity of a lifetime. I now know that it is a lifetime of opportunity. Thank you, God, for preparing me so that I was able to accept this gift for what it is.

So you see, God's plan for us does not always coincide with what we want or where we want to go. I've learned in the last ten years that His plan is infinitely greater than we can ever imagine it to be. Mark Twain said, "The two best days of your life are the day you are born and the day you find out why." I personally found some of the "why" through the lessons I learned going through some of these experiences. Laura has helped me to discover some of the reasons I am here. Being part of the

Ziglar Legacy Certified Trainers family has brought me further down the road to finding my "why." I look forward to learning more of "why" I exist, because I now know it will be so much more than I can imagine, as long as I trust in God's plan for me.

God bless. ⌒

KEN GRANT

Ken Grant spent the first three months of his life in infant ICU as he just couldn't wait to come into this world and spread the message of faith and success. He grew up in Aurora, Colorado, and saw Zig Ziglar speak in person at the tender age of 12. His father was a salesman and he, along with Zig, instilled all the great qualities of a salesman in Ken as he grew up.

Ken graduated from high school near the top of his class and earned a bachelor of science degree in Microbiology from Colorado State University (with the idea of entering the School of Veterinary Medicine—a long-time goal). Ken proceeded to become a salesman, eventually ending up as a successful, open, honest, and faithful account executive for a leading mortgage company. Sales was his calling and passion, thanks to Zig, and microbiology was just a small detour.

As a Zig Ziglar Legacy Certified Trainer, Ken continues to pass along his passion to succeed to all his clients, friends, and family. He first believed that Zig Ziglar Legacy Certified training was the opportunity of a lifetime, but, after completing the training, Ken knows that it actually created a lifetime of opportunities for himself and anyone to whom he passes on Zig's time-proven principles.

Ken Grant
720-344-4196
Ken.Grant_Ziglar@comcast.net

CONNECT THE DOTS

By Nikki Ivey

WRITING A CHAPTER about your life isn't always the easiest thing to do. I have written a couple of pieces that I have enjoyed writing, but this piece will be my very first to get published. The first thought that came to mind when I was given the opportunity to write a chapter in a book, together with some of the most amazing people I have ever met, was excitement. And then, the things I planned to write about became even more exciting because I have always had such a deep passion for helping others through my experiences.

As I began writing this chapter, I had an outline of my life in front of me. I started having reservations because I was going to have to confront some things that happened in my life that I haven't really dealt with—and maybe didn't want to revisit. How can I put things down on paper about my experiences and the wonderful things that have unfolded because of what I have been through? How am I going to portray events that raise an eyebrow to some—or more so, who will even care? I proceeded to write about what happened in my life, and I put a certain twist to the story to show you, the person taking time to read about events in someone else's life, how everything eventually comes together if we just take some time, iron out details, and figure out how things fit together. I want to share with you how I made sense of my life's events, how I have overcome obstacles, how I used what happened to figure out the direction of my life—and I want to help you to do the same.

We go through life not really knowing what we are doing or where we are going, but it is up to us to figure out where we came from and where we are heading. What makes us the people we are, the parents we become, with careers we choose, the places where we live or even the places we go on vacation? We all have so many different paths, and we all end up in different areas with different beliefs, understandings, and so on. How did we get where we are today? What direction will our lives take? What is our purpose? Have we missed the mark? What can we do to get back on track?

Here's my story.

My childhood started in the small town of Hobbs, New Mexico. I had two of the most amazing parents and grandparents in the world. Although my parents were the most amazing parents a girl could have, they ended up divorcing when I was three years old. I didn't realize the impact of a divorce at the time, but the event ended up affecting me later in life. I was fortunate to still be able to be around both parents and sets of grandparents regularly. I didn't pay much attention to my parents' divorce because soon after the divorce I was sexually abused by a non-family member, and the abuse continued for many years.

Being as young as I was when the abuse started, I was unaware of the abnormality of the events. Even though I belonged to a divorced family and constant abuse was going on, I had the most amazing childhood. Let me explain. I went to an amazing school, Taylor Elementary, and I had amazing friends, coupled with incredible teachers year after year. I could hardly wait for each day to come so that I could get to school and see all my wonderful friends and all the very patient teachers as well.

You see, we were an "entertaining bunch" of students. Teachers knew years in advance that "the group" was coming. We were all so close, laughing all the time and loving each other more than words can ever explain. And to this day, we have such a bond that it's indescribable with words. In fact, just a couple of months ago, I put a picture on my Facebook page saying something along the lines of, "You never forget the neighborhood kids you grew up with," and within a couple of days, there were over two thousand comments. We ended up creating a page so we could all always stay in touch.

I had one teacher in particular who always hugged me and made me laugh. She was so upbeat and on the ball; her energy would liven up any room, and I always wanted to grow up and be just like her—Mrs. Chaney. You see, although there were some details of my childhood that were, let's say, less than ideal, so I focused on my amazing parents, grandparents, friends, and sweet Mrs. Chaney. Even though some things seemed difficult to deal with, there was always a light in the storm, and God's love for me remained the same.

Years went on, and some of my friends moved to the same junior high I went to, and some went to other schools. But it seemed as if there was always at least one person in my life who gave me that little positive nudge to keep going or inspire me in some way. Junior high is a world all its own, but again, I still had the most amazing friends. I was in the band and the choir; I was on the student council and an honor student.

Things on the outside appeared to be fantastic in my life, but at the age of fourteen I became pregnant.

I chose not to tell anyone because, to be honest, I had no idea what to do. I guess in my fourteen-year-old mind, it couldn't be possible to be pregnant at that age. Well, as the months went on, I began to show. My closest friends knew first, and, as things in junior high normally go, word got around fast. My mother heard the news from someone and took me to the doctor to confirm. She was quiet but supportive. I'm not really sure how my father found out, but he came around too. My grandparents were so amazingly awesome and loving, especially my grandma Meme, who had married my grandfather when I was younger.

It was an emotional time because some of my friends were not allowed to be around me anymore, and even the church I attended at the time told me I was not allowed to be in the youth group any longer. Funny thing about being young, I had a determination about me because of the support that I had from my friends and of course from those few people who encouraged me in junior high, such as Principal Jim Gardner who said I could do anything if I put my mind to it, and one lady at church, Sonja Isbell, who came into the nursery where I was working and told me she had heard I was pregnant. When I went to put my head down, she told me I would be the most incredible mother in the world. Everyone has trials and tribulations, but what you choose to focus on will determine the direction of your life. And through that time, God's love for me remained the same.

Parenthood arrived. I was fifteen years old, a freshman in junior high, and I had the world ahead of me. Of course, I have to say that I became the mother of one amazing young man. He was born special; he had the brightest eyes in the world and held his head up at the hospital and looked around. I knew without a single doubt that this young man was going to be a world changer. This baby was my angel, and because I got the honor of being his mother, I would work hard to provide a life for him.

My mother and I decided that we would work together to raise this incredible young man. He more than blessed both of our lives. It wasn't always easy for my mother, you see; she was not only a single mother to me, but now she was also a single grandmother to my son. But the love that we both had for him was unstoppable.

I moved out of my mother's house when my son was still a baby, and even though I was only fifteen, I worked as hard as I could for him. He stayed at my mother's house because the places where I stayed were unfit for my son, and many times I was homeless and hardly getting by. I had to make a decision to do what was best for my son and not worry about what others thought. As soon as I got on my feet, got a steady job, a vehicle, and a decent place to live, my son started staying with me full time. The years went on and I continued to work as hard as I could to not only provide for this amazing young man who deserved the world but to also be the best mother that I knew how to be at the time.

We lived next door to an amazing family who took us in as their own and made us part of their family. I learned so much over these years of working and attending college, and I relied heavily on my neighbor and second mother, Margie Dale Henry. We talked for hours each day about everything. I went to school during the week and worked twelve-hour shifts on the weekends for five years, and when I came home on Sunday evenings, I went next door to a huge family and a hot plate.

Margie Dale has always been like a mother to me. She believed in me and always gave me advice and courage to keep working toward my goals. To this day, I refer back to her many words of wisdom and views on life. I call her mom, and I love her and my entire next-door family. There will always be outstanding people in this world who will love you unconditionally, spend time to get to know the real you, and encourage you to be your best self. Through these times, God's love for me remained the same.

Somehow, I continued on in college, worked hard as a full-time janitor and a loan officer. I mowed lawns, worked for friends, had different jobs at the local hospital and then a medical center until I finished college and became a teacher. I went on to get my first teaching job at my favorite school, Taylor Elementary. Again, there were a couple of people who were always pulling for me during this time. I had the finest example of leadership while working at that school, a man by the name of Freddie Salgado, who was the principal. Mr. Salgado led that school with integrity and class. He loved the students and the teachers and always appreciated our hard work. Mr. Salgado believed in me and told me to remember that someone is always watching to see you rise and fall, so always give them something great to talk about.

The other person at that school was none other than my favorite teacher as a child, Mrs. Chaney. She had been my saving grace as a child and was now my saving grace as a fellow teacher in the same school. I was working at a medical center and student teaching at the same time, and somehow I got my own class of amazing second graders at the end of my student teaching. I will never forget the day that Mr. Salgado announced on the intercom to welcome the newest member of the staff to Taylor Elementary. I was standing in the hall and heard the announcement, and I began to cry. This was such a pivotal moment in my life. The first phone call I made was to my grandmother to tell her the news; and she couldn't understand a word I was saying.

As you can imagine, there have been so many people along the way who said I could never—and would never—make it or make anything of myself. I have even had a principal tell me I wasn't meant to be a teacher. All I focused on were the people who believed in me, the great things they said, and knowing who I was. Everything else was simply an interpretation of someone they never spent the time to get to know and understand. And through all that, God's love for me remained the same.

Years went on; my son grew up so fast. We moved to Odessa, Texas, to be closer to my dad and his parents. We really just wanted a change to a bigger city and different opportunities. My son was now in junior high and I continued teaching. I became restless with teaching because I have never had just one job; I also felt that there was more that I could do. I think it goes without saying that, being a school teacher, I needed more income.

I had the opportunity to get into a couple of marketing companies part-time and absolutely loved presenting and inspiring people to make changes in their lives, no matter what it might be. I loved traveling in my rolling university, and on one of the audio CD's that I listened to I heard a story about a flea and how if you put a flea in a jar the flea will soon start only jumping to the height of the lid. I couldn't remember the entire story, but the story completely intrigued me. I did research on fleas and came up with my own version of the story.

When I made my presentation, I started telling people that a flea could jump from four to six feet high. Now isn't that gross? But if you were to take the flea and put it in a jar and put the lid on, the flea would try to jump its regular height of four to six feet, but it would begin to bump its head. It would figure out really soon that it should only jump to the height of the lid. Then, if you were to take the lid off the jar, and take the flea out, it would continue to jump to the height of the lid because he was conditioned not to jump as high as it could. I went on to explain that the flea would continue to jump to the height of the lid until something were to happen to cause the flea to jump to its forgotten potential.

I continued to present and talk in front of other people, and soon the information I kept presenting about people not reaching their full potential stopped me in my tracks. For years, I had felt restless with teaching. Teaching for me is much bigger than showing up and teaching the alphabet. I invest my heart and my time into developing good people for the future, but I have had a soul-tugging feeling that I am meant to do something more. But what was it that I was supposed to do?

I do know one thing: You can't figure out where you are going if you don't know where you've been. So whatever was next, I knew one thing: God's love for me remained the same.

You see, we go through life not really totally understanding what we are doing or where we are going, but then one thing leads to another and one or two people stand out from a crowd and encourage you in some way to keep going. I looked back on the events that took place in my life and connected the dots from one thing to another. I have always had amazing friends who have loved me unconditionally. The love and support of my parents and grandparents got me through the toughest times in my life and, even though my parents' divorce affected me later in life, the positives that came from growing up and being raised by a very strong, God-fearing single mother with an incredible work ethic gave me the confidence that I would without a doubt be able to be a strong single mother as well.

I have a bond with my father that is unbreakable. My father has supported me, stood by me, and loved me more than anyone is able to love someone, and I feel the same about him. He is my security and my hero, and I have learned how to love from him. Being abused as a child and in my teens gave me the insight to help others who have gone through abusive situations as well. Loving to go to school each day even though divorce and abuse was a factor gave me the desire to become a teacher and to be there for children who might have unknown struggles at home. Being part of "the group" at Taylor Elementary gave me understanding and love for a challenge with the students I would have someday.

Teaching shows me how to live my life like a child who loves unconditionally and doesn't allow anything to ruin their day. Sometimes, I think I learn way more from my students then they ever learn from me. Becoming a mother at an early age taught me not to judge others, because you really never know what is going on in people's lives. And that amazing young man whose mother I am blessed to be gave me drive like no other to get on my feet, make something of myself, and lead him by the example my parents led me. Moving out at such an early age and struggling to get by made me work very hard and never take anything for granted. To this day I wake up in the morning and thank God for the home that I have, running water, electricity, food to eat, and a vehicle to drive.

Working my way through college helped me learn how to multi task and always keep my goals in mind. More so than anything, I have written that what got me through each phase of my life was the fact that there were incredible people who showed me unconditional love and support. And they had leadership skills that I would work so very hard to mimic in my life to help give someone else the same positive nudge that so many have given me on my journey. Everything has led me to the point where I can use what experiences I have had in my life to help other people. So that is exactly what this chapter is for.

My question is twofold:

- What are the events in your life that have led you to where you are right now?
- And have you connected all the dots to create a complete picture?

At this point in my life, I have had five dots to connect, and I start imagining the picture that the five dots could create—and of course I find that five dots can make a star. Anyone who knows me knows how I always have some type of star on me at all times. My acronym for star is "Someone Talented Always Rising." What does "rising" mean to me? Rising to the occasion, rising after failing, rising to a higher calling, rising to stand up for what you believe in, rising time after time when you are knocked down.

My calling is now clear: I should do what I love—and that is to help people connect their dots. But how? I want to be a public speaker, and I am most comfortable in front of a crowd of people. One event leads to another, and before you know it my son turns eighteen years old. I have been an incredibly successful teacher for ten years, and I find myself in Plano, Texas, at Ziglar headquarters becoming a Ziglar Certified Legacy Trainer! I get the opportunity to fine-tune the flea story from the Ziglars themselves! I am not sure exactly what I was expecting when I walked through those doors, but immediately I felt like I had been there before. I felt a love and embrace that I have never felt from other people in my life. Every person I met that day I felt as if I had known for years.

The Ziglar team and all the people who were there to become ZLCers (Ziglar Legacy Certified) quickly formed a bond, and we all went through the Ziglar classes together as a whole. We grew not only as people, but we grew together; we had a sense of purpose like never before. As the week went on, we laughed, cried, broke down, and built each other back up; and in the evenings we worked on self-development planners that gave us clear vision for our days ahead. I have never felt so invested, so trusted, and so honored.

Friday came quickly. The week was almost over and it was a bittersweet feeling. I knew the experience was almost over and it was back to the real world after that. I couldn't get enough pictures, hugs, videos—and then it was graduation time. And there I was, for the first time in my life, I was surrounded in a room full of people who actually loved and accepted me. And for the first time, I accepted myself—and I was getting pinned by Tom and Julie Ziglar. I was overcome with emotion and couldn't stop crying, because they trusted me with the most precious gift they could ever give to someone and that was to go out into this world and carry on their father's legacy.

What an incredible honor! You see, you will be placed exactly where you are supposed to be; you will be surrounded by exactly who you are supposed to be surrounded by. Just don't quit. Your next chapter is right around the corner—and through all that, God's love for me remained the same.

Driving back from my life-changing experience at Ziglar headquarters, I began to have more clarity about my life's direction. I came to the conclusion that all this stuff that has happened to me in my life has never been about me at all. This life has always been about how I can use my experiences to help other people get through what they are going through and to encourage others to keep going. And God's love for me remained the same.

To be continued ...

I know that every person has had trials and tribulations and has overcome things that knocked me completely down. I have felt so alone, but I can't help but think about what my mentor, Zig Ziglar, says. He says that it is so important that everyone write a book about their life to give them clear understanding about themselves. And it does just that. Writing down the events of your life helps you get a clear vision of what has happened and how it all works together to create a big picture.

I want to encourage you to start small, make of list of the people in your life who have given you a positive nudge to get through to your big picture. Go through the events in your life; see how they have led to other events; and connect the dots. Really spend time giving this some thought and writing things down. When you are done connecting the dots, ask yourself the following questions:

- Have the dots in your life created the picture you have wanted?
- Is there a way to rearrange the dots to make a different picture?
- Who are the people who have given you positive nudges?
- Are you giving people positive nudges to someday connect their dots?

I encourage you to take the time to connect the dots in your life. Thank the people who have given you the encouraging nudges you have needed to become a person who does the nudging to others. You never truly know who you are or what the direction of your life is until you look at the big picture you create by connecting the dots. There is no time like the present. It is a gift. Take time to connect the dots. ✑

NIKKI IVEY

Nikki Ivey is a passionate, determined speaker dedicated to helping others overcome obstacles and realize their full potential in big ways. With her experience as a single mother, teacher, college student, business owner, and now a Ziglar Legacy Certified Trainer, Nikki has the natural ability to connect, inspire and motivate others to reach higher and go farther in their personal and professional lives.

Nikki's journey began at the tender age of fifteen when she became a Mother. Despite the challenges, Nikki worked hard to finish school, go on to college and begin a successful teaching career. Her love for others motivated her to look for additional opportunities to serve and she soon became an entrepreneur making a living helping others get what they want out of life.

Nikki is on a mission to help people work through life's setbacks and design the life they want. Now, as a Ziglar Legacy Certified Trainer, she is taking her message of hope to even more audiences around the country to help motivate, inspire and encourage them to live their best life too!

ziglarcertified.com/nikkiivey
nikkiivey.net
nikkiiveyzlc@yahoo.com

HOW SEVEN STEPS TO GOAL SETTING HELPED SAVE MY LIFE

By Karl Kispert

THERE ARE SO many tools, techniques, and, yes, shady tricks in the marketplace today to assist people in losing weight, reaching a fitness level, or improving their health. My story is about a proven method that was built around behavior and not a pill that might enhance this or reduce that. I found that setting goals and following a goals program developed by Zig Ziglar changed who I am inside and how I think about health and wellness. With this goals program, daily motivation, and inspiration from Zig Ziglar's countless stories, quotes, videos, books, and CDs, I have been able to define for myself a new, healthier life.

Remember three nine nine point eight—I will get to this a little later in this chapter.

I was introduced to my mentor, Zig Ziglar, in December of 2007 when I found myself without a job, laid off from the company that I thought I would retire from. I met Zig on a bookstore shelf while I was looking for some prose to lift my spirit, something that would motivate me and inspire me and let me know things were going to be all right.

I picked up a book entitled *Better Than Good*, and I asked myself, *Who is this guy?* and *Why does he have a "better than good" life?* I figured all I had to do was read it from cover to cover and perhaps magically my life would be the way it used to be—with a job and the ability to support myself and my family. I felt I was a failure even though I told myself it had been a business decision to remove six of the top management officials at the company. I later came to realize something very valuable that Zig always said: "Failure is an event, not a person."

Over the years I enrolled in "Automobile University" (AU)—you may be an alumnus or are currently enrolled there: education via CDs or podcasts while driving to or from your destination. My primary professor was Zig Ziglar; however, there were several other professors I took classes from. But he was my favorite. My major at AU was motivation and inspiration, with a minor in goal setting and achievement. It was my minor that I want to discuss here in the next few pages.

Before I do, I must cover two very important foundational aspects of my life for you to understand. You see, three days after my sixth birthday my father lost his battle with cancer (Cancer sucks!) and became a guardian in heaven. I say guardian because as I grew up on the south side of Scranton, Pennsylvania, my neighbors told me stories of my father and how he took care of others in the neighborhood, whether he knew them or not. He was the "go to" guy when people needed help, regardless what the problem was. If it was to help fix a lawn mower engine or replace a kitchen light fixture, he was always there to lend a hand.

The owner of Buscarini's Pizza told me many stories of my father and on many occasions said that when the "wrong element" showed up on the streets of the south side, my father would patrol the streets with an ax handle. Standing six foot three and weighing two hundred and sixty-five pounds, I am sure he was quite the figure. He was intimidating without the ax handle, but to those who knew my father he was the gentlest of giants. I think he must have listened to Zig because he learned that "You can have everything in life you want if you will just help enough other people get what they want."

The second important foundational element was my faith and devotion to St. Mary's Assumption Church and the Catholic faith. Growing up and attending grade school and high school, many men from the parish made sure I stayed on the right track, patted my shoulder when I needed a father figure to do it, and provided me words of encouragement. I knew that they were messengers of Jesus—and my father—helping me navigate my early life.

Growing up I had two very important figures in my life, two women who shaped who I am today. They taught me right from wrong, good from evil—all the things you would expect from a mother and a grandmother—but they taught me so much more. (I am going to say nice things about them now because my mother may read this book and I still look for brownie points from her and my grandmother, who's sitting with my father above.)

Charlotte, my mother, was left to raise three boys on her own. At the beginning, after my father died, it was very difficult—go figure, right! Taking care of an eleven-, six-, and three-year-old posed many challenges, as you can imagine. She had a deep devotion to her faith and religion and a huge support team from the neighbors, parish, the local Sears store where my father worked, and one lady in particular—her mother, my grandmother. Mary Russell, "Nana" to most people, was there, always. She herself knew hardship; she had raised three children alone after her husband decided to leave her one day.

There are a couple of life lessons that were planted into my gray matter early on in my life and reinforced over the years. My mother was a living example of "You can do it," "Don't give up, ever," "Do the right thing," "Treat others as you would expect them to treat you," "Life IS fair—you just have to look for it," and "Set goals and work toward them." She must have known Zig as well. Raising three boys and putting each one through college, one at Villanova and two at the University of Scranton, was a monumental achievement in itself. We all worked together to accomplish that goal. We did without for so many years to make sure we all had enough and received our college diploma.

My grandmother also instilled many important traits, but she did it in her own special way. We called them "Maryisms." "You will live until you die," and "Don't give up the ship"—the lesson of persistence. "You have legs up to your ass, use them"—the lesson of hard work and don't take the easy way out. "Pull over. I know that person"—this takes a little explanation. You see, when I would drive my grandmother anywhere and everywhere, and she saw an elderly person walking with bags or a cart, she would say "Karly, pull over. I know that person." So I would pull over, and she would jump out of the car like a kid in front of an ice cream store. She would say, "Hello, my name is Mary Russell, and my grandson and I are going to give you a ride to where you are going." I came to realize that ninety-plus percent of the people for whom we pulled over had no idea who this white-haired elderly woman was, but not one refused the ride. I became the taxi service for many who could not afford a ride.

My grandmother instilled in me over and over again through this one action that "You can have everything in life you want, if you will just help enough other people get what they want." She wanted to help EVERYONE. And she sure tried hard: by making dozens of afghans for the needy and elderly in retirement homes, by delivering homemade bread to people who just needed a warm loaf to enrich their meals, or by inviting strangers into her home for a warm meal. She wanted to help everyone—and she practically did! Her generosity and sincere kindness never stopped. She touched hundreds of people through her ninety-two years on this earth, and I am sure Jesus and Saint Peter have matching afghans in heaven. This trait of kindness and giving is one that's at the core of my DNA, and I am proud and humbled to carry on some of Mary Russell's traditions.

I am one hundred percent confident that the reason I am who I am today is because of these two selfless women who took care of others before themselves. I say thank you; however, I wonder if I say it enough. So I will say it here in print, "Thank you, Mom and Nana, for who you are and how you have inspired me to be a better person. I LOVE YOU!"

Now, let me get back to three hundred nine nine point eight. It wasn't long ago that I looked at myself in a mirror. It wasn't long ago that I climbed a flight of stairs and looked around for more oxygen to fill my lungs. It wasn't that long ago that I realized playing with my kids might kill me. It wasn't that long ago I wanted something different in my life. I set a goal to be FIT at 50. You see, like many people I have been on the roller coaster of life, weight going up, weight going down, weight going up, weight going down—oh, and then one of those upside down loops just to throw that into the mix of life. I have probably lost over two thousand pounds over the decades. My weight was no accident, I consciously ate the food. Someone told me that I did not get this size by eating celery sticks—I still love her.

I had set my goal before—FIT by 50. But I was being plagued by FTI, "Failure to Implement." I needed something with accountability. So I decided to try Weight Watchers.

When I started my journey with Weight Watchers, I knew I was morbidly obese—my doctors had been telling me so for more than 20 years. But I thought, *What's a few pounds on a 6'6" frame when my blood pressure, sugar, heart rate, and cholesterol are normal?* I had lost weight before, but it wasn't for long, and it was never for me. I would do it because other people told me I needed to. I never admitted that I was in a health crisis. I would start a new fad diet, always on a Monday, and by Wednesday I would start slipping back into old habits. Sometimes, the diet would work, and I would lose 20 or 25 pounds, but it was always short-lived, and the weight found its way back. Finally, reality hit me when I couldn't walk up a flight of stairs without getting winded. My legs were retaining water; I couldn't keep up with my two children; and my clothes increased by two inches every couple of months. I knew that sixty was supposed to be someone's age, not their waist size. I needed to kick the old habits and replace them with something new—and I had to do it right away!

I sat in the parking lot, and then, after several minutes of hesitation, I decided to have faith in God and walked into the Weight Watchers building. Then I saw it, the bane of my existence—the scale. I asked myself, *Do I really want to get on that humbling device?* It was, after all, the one thing I had avoided for years. Did I really want that woman behind the desk to know something so personal about me that even my wife didn't know? "Okay, you can step on the scale," I heard from the lady with a smile on her face sitting at the table in front of me. I took a deep breath and got on. I was not ready for the number I heard—I was ashamed, embarrassed, mortified, and disappointed. My weight was three hundred ninety-nine point eight pounds. My heart skipped a beat. I went into instant denial, thinking, *This scale is obviously not calibrated properly.* Of course, just another excuse. This time I knew I could do it; this time it was for me; and on the walk back to my car I committed to my family and myself.

Now you understand the three nine nine point eight. I am sure at some point prior to my weigh-in that day I had gone over four hundred pounds, but officially it was three nine nine point eight. However, things were different now. I knew going into this journey that I was going to use a variety of tools, which included a solid plan. I was going to set the goal and work hard to accomplish it. I was going to be motivated and inspired every day. Guess what: back to automobile university and reading books by my mentor, Zig Ziglar.

Zig created a seven-step procedure for goal setting. They include:

1. Identify your goal
2. Benefits from reaching this goal
3. Major obstacles and mountains to climb to reach this goal
4. Skills or knowledge required to reach this goal
5. Individuals, groups, companies and organizations to work with to reach this goal
6. Plan of action to reach this goal
7. Completion date

I had the motivation, I had the inspiration. And now I had a proven goal-setting tool—and not just a tool, but a process on setting goals and achieving them. I was ready. I want to take you through each step and explain how I applied it to my goal and how you might be able to apply it to your goals.

Step 1: Identify your goal

Your goal needs to be clearly identifiable, and preferably measurable. My goal was to become healthier and embrace a lifestyle of healthy habits including regular exercise for both my mind and body. I knew that anything south of three nine nine point eight was heading in the right direction. I needed the assistance of my physician to oversee my journey and together we could set a realistic goal, one that we were both happy with—and we did.

Two four five point zero—that was my target weight, my goal. I placed that number inside my brain in the same area where I used to think about when I would get my next burger or snack. I wanted to be sure it was in the forefront of my daily thought. I wrote it down on a Post-it, and guess what: I posted it! The goal: two four five point zero. A goal that I would be able to measure daily if I wanted to and one that I would be happy with along with my doctor. I will never strive to be my ideal weight according to some insurance chart. I take my direction from the doctor who knows me best.

Step 2: Benefits from realizing this goal

The more benefits you can write down, and read to yourself often, the more motivation and inspiration you will generate within yourself. The more you tell yourself these are the true benefits, the more you will realize that they are possible. There is a saying: "You are what you think about." If I am going to think about where the next fast-food joint is located so that I can stop by and grab a shake and some fries, then I will stop for a shake and some fries—and then some! If I think about watching a television show at night and what snack I will have with it, I will do just that. That is how I thought for years and years; they were my goals and, unfortunately, I exceeded them ALL. Not Good!

I needed to change the way I was thinking and what I was thinking about. I needed to generate positive self-talk and change what I was putting into my brain on a daily basis. I needed to focus on the benefits and think about the benefits. I needed to focus on the benefits of healthy eating, exercise, how I would feel, how I would appear to others, and so on. I created a list of positive self-statements; they were, and continue to be, in my daily thoughts. I call them the "I'm Gonna Club." Here they are:

I'm gonna...be healthier for me and my family

I'm gonna...be a good example for my family

I'm gonna...play longer and harder with my children

I'm gonna...tag my kids when we are playing tag

I'm gonna...feel better about myself

I'm gonna...walk long distances and not get out of breath

I'm gonna...climb hundreds of steps and not feel like I am going to die

I'm gonna...have more energy than the energizer bunny

I'm gonna...throw away all of my clothes that are too big

I'm gonna...buy a new wardrobe and enjoy shopping for a smaller size

I'm gonna...be at a healthy weight for someone my height, not someone 14 feet tall

I'm gonna...reduce my risk of heart disease, diabetes and any other disease associated with obesity

I'm gonna...shop at the tall clothing store not the big and tall store

I'm gonna...inspire others and show them that it is really possible to lose weight and keep it off

I'm gonna...be the object of attention for reasons other than being the largest in the room

I'm gonna...have a before and after picture that I can be proud of and is still current twenty years from today

I'm gonna...remove the word morbid obesity from my language

I'm gonna...be comfortable on airplanes at least from a width perspective

I'm gonna...sit in a chair and not have to worry about it breaking

I'm gonna...share my success with all who will listen

I'm gonna...read a scale by looking straight down and it not screaming for me to get off

I'm gonna...be physically fit, exercise daily and enjoy it

I'm gonna...say that there was once a time when I was overweight

I'm gonna...wear an exam gown at the doctor's office without my butt being exposed (ICU)

I'm gonna...look professional in a suit

I'm gonna...actually have a bath towel cover all of me? Refer to doctor's office above

I'm gonna...sit at a booth in a restaurant and be comfortable

I'm gonna...have fun and enjoy every day as a healthy person

I'm gonna...feel ALIVE

I'm gonna...BE

By visualizing my benefits, my motivation and self-inspiration engine runs at 100 percent every day. It really works—try it!

Step 3: Major obstacles and mountains to climb to reach this goal

If you list all the obstacles standing between you and your goal, then you can learn how to overcome them. All the obstacles you list will not be a surprise when they occur and are less likely to throw you off course. I listed the following:

- **Love** – I love food. The problem is that I love too many portions of food. My weakness was always bread and sweets—one big happy German.

- **Stress** – I am not sure if stress triggered eating with me or slowed my eating habits down. It seemed that during my life I could attribute it to both.

- **Exercise** – This is not rocket science, you know. The more the body is in motion the more calories you burn, the more your body is at rest the fewer calories you burn.

- **Time** – Time to reflect on my goals, on my dreams, on ME. The older you get, the more complicated it seems to manage family, work, and what I need.

Step 4: Skills or knowledge required to reach this goal.

List what you need to know to accomplish this goal. This is a very important step because you need some special tools in your toolbox. I had to learn how to eat healthy, understand why protein was so important, and why H2O was critical to sustain what I wanted to do. I basically had to learn healthy habits from scratch. I was able to accomplish this step in three ways. First was the program I started with Weight Watchers— lots of tools there. In addition, I started using the membership I had to the local health club. I realized that tool was rusty, but I took it out, polished it some, and started to use it regularly. As you know, tools that are used regularly turn into precision machines, and I was witnessing that first-hand.

After using these tools for several months I felt something lacking. I wanted to visit the tool department and look for a new tool that would get me closer to my goal and build a stronger me. I found that tool at the health club in the trainer aisle. This leads to step 5.

Step 5: Individuals, groups, companies, and organizations to work with to reach this goal

There are many resources that you can utilize; you just have to start. As I mentioned in Step 4 above, I was in the trainer aisle, and this young woman came up to me and introduced herself by saying with a huge smile, "Hi, my name is Rebecca Koons." She was bobbing from one foot to the other and being very nice. I think they learn that in trainer school—you know what I mean; they say all the right things and smile a lot. Rebecca asked me what I wanted to accomplish, and she said that she could help me reach my goal. Did she also study the principles of Zig Ziglar?

I soon came to realize that her idea of a workout was a combination of something used by the NAVY Seals and something used by those training for a Spartan Race. Over the next several months, with many very long one-hour sessions, I found myself getting closer and closer to my goal. I will say it was challenging at times; some days I loved Rebecca, and others, well let's just say I did not. At the end of every session, regardless of my feelings, we exchanged high fives and words of encouragement. I came to learn a new vocabulary, word such as burpies, lunges, planks, and battle ropes.

There was one philosophy that Rebecca used with me that I learned from Zig, and this is: "and then some." She would have me do 40 pushups "and then some," stay on the treadmill for an hour "and then some," work with the battle ropes for ten minutes "and then some." After a short time of this, it simply became the natural thing to do. It is another example of "You are what you think about." One more thing that Rebecca did early on was to send out motivational texts to me which continued to fuel the engine.

Step 6: Plan of action to reach this goal

After identifying my goal, writing down the benefits of reaching my goal, realizing obstacles and mountains that I needed to climb, acquiring the skills and knowledge to reach my goal and aligning with individuals and companies to work with, I set a plan. I wrote the plan down, read the plan every day, believed in the plan, committed to the plan, and, guess what, I started to live it one day at a time. If I had a bad day for whatever reason, I did not stop. I followed what Zig said: "Yesterday ended last night and today is a brand new day—and it is yours." Most days were met with small successes, and those small successes helped me get so much closer to my goal.

I referred to my plan like I refer to my GPS on a long trip heading toward a new destination. The GPS has the entire route mapped out, and if I take a wrong turn it will reroute me very quickly to make sure I am back on track and headed toward my destination. The plan of action is laid out, and it's there to remind me if I get lost or off track and need to be rerouted. I know that if you contemplate your action plan, create your action plan, believe in your action plan, and live your action plan, you will reach your goal. This brings me to yet another important philosophy of Zig's: "You were born to win. But to be the winner you must plan to win and prepare to win. Then, and only then, can you legitimately expect to win." This is YOUR action plan.

Step 7: Completion date

Back to the GPS analogy I used above: You know that there is an estimated time of arrival and that to ensure you and I stay on course, a completion date must be set. Sometimes it is difficult to set a date far into the future, but you must do it. It absolutely helps with accountability, and you will want to know where the milestones are on your time line.

As I reflect on this goal-setting process that Zig came up with, I can attest to you today that it did help save my life. I encourage you to use this process for whatever goal you want to accomplish. Live it daily, embrace it, and make it YOURS. Zig always said: "There is no elevator to success ...you have to take the stairs." Accomplishing your goals will take time. I assure you that if you follow these seven steps you will cross the finish line. One final thing that Zig taught me: "Anything worth doing is worth doing poorly until you learn to do it well." Go and master your goal-setting process—YOU deserve it! ∽

KARL KISPERT

I was born and raised in Scranton, Pennsylvania, in a loving home and community that laid the foundation of who I am today. My first job was as a paperboy at 14, and I have been working since—that is a long time! I have over 26 years of corporate experience, all in some capacity interacting with people. This foundation has allowed and equipped me to provide the type of personal and team coaching and training that will deliver meaningful results. Zig Ziglar was my mentor, and I am so fortunate to consider myself one of those millions who have been touched. Everyone has their own "story" and reasons why they look to Zig Ziglar for motivation and inspiration. My story was about finding a solid goal-setting process to guide me on my health and fitness journey. I found more than the best way to set meaningful goals and how to achieve them; I also found out how to build a stronger ME along with so much motivation and inspiration.

I am so proud and humble to have been chosen by the Ziglar family to carry on the legacy of their father, Zig Ziglar. At the present time, there are only 57 Ziglar Legacy Certified Trainers and Coaches worldwide. I have made it my personal and professional mission to promote the Ziglar Legacy as the most effective, balanced, and proven system for achieving true success in life. If you want to experience a "Better than Good Life," I encourage you to contact me directly at 973.229.5566. I always prefer a person-to-person call; however, you can also reach me at Karl@kispertgroup.com or visit my websites at:

www.ziglarcertified.com/karlkispert, or
www.kispertgroup.com/services/motivating

to learn more about me and how we can work together. If you take the first step and contact me, we can start this unique experience together.

EXPONENTIAL IMPACT

By James McLamb

HOW CAN SOMEONE you have never met, never spoken to, or never seen in person, impact your life in a dramatic way? Outside of having a relationship with Jesus Christ and then following his teachings, could any one person's teachings help shape your life's philosophy? YES! Yes, they can. For me, that person was Zig Ziglar. He is someone whom I have never met personally, and whose teaching I was only exposed to from others who had heard him speak live. Ziglar was a hero to me, teaching common-sense ideas on how to reach the top. Three times I was taught what he taught from others, and those three times dramatically changed the course of my life.

You were designed for accomplishment, engineered for success, and endowed with the seeds of greatness. —Zig Ziglar

As a freshman entering high school, I had what most fourteen-year-olds have, a very low self-image. Now, don't get me wrong, I did not think negatively of myself or that I was incapable of accomplishing great things. It's just that I had no idea how to get where I wanted to go. Plus, I was shorter than most of my peers, a late bloomer when it came to athletics or fitness, and I was struggling to have the courage to take advantage of the opportunities presented to me. Deep inside, I knew there was more to me than what others were seeing—I knew I had potential. However, in ninth grade there were not a lot of positive reinforcements coming from any direction. My fellow classmates were struggling with their own self-esteem issues; the teachers were positive, but they had 75 or more students to deal with each day. Even though my family loved me, they either did not see self-confidence problems or did not know what to do to help.

So my entire freshman I struggled to find my place and to discover who I was. At the end of the year, a teacher saw potential in me and gave me a freshman class award in leadership for the Future Farmers of America (FFA) chapter at my school. This was a turning point. Finally, someone else was seeing some potential in me. The teacher urged me to attend the state FFA leadership camp that summer. The most important decision I made in my life thus far was convincing my parents to let me go.

At camp I was one of the youngest participants. I was shy and introverted, keeping mostly to myself and to those from my own school's chapter. Each day in the morning, we attended sessions on public speaking, business etiquette, and leadership development. One class really hit home with me.

I do not remember to this day who conducted the session, but the session leaders discussed 15 steps to a healthy self-image. What I heard that morning amazed me. They first discussed signs of low self-esteem and asked us to identify any signs we saw in ourselves. "The student with a poor self-image," we heard, "will not confront the teacher over a poor grade, even when they deserve a better one." Hey, that is me, I thought—I was starting to pay attention. "The student with a poor self-image can't stand it if they suspect someone is laughing at them and sometimes withdraws from activities to prevent that from happening." Now, they really had my attention. It was as if someone had fed them information about me. As they described each aspect of a poor self-image, I began to see patterns in my own life. I eagerly awaited the steps to a healthy self-image.

Although they went over 15 steps that day, only three made a strong impression. **First:** "Take Inventory of the skills and talents you have." At first, I thought that wasn't much, but, as I wrote down what I believed my skills and talents were, I recognized that I possessed much more than I realized. As I took inventory of my "assets," I amazed myself at what I had honestly listed. "Hey, this is awesome!" I thought. I am worth far more than I even knew. I could not wait until I could use these newly discovered skills and talents. Yes, I was shorter than most boys my age, but I was faster than most. I knew I could compete athletically if I capitalized on this talent. Yes, I still mumbled when I spoke in public, but I was not afraid of public speaking, so, therefore, I knew I could refine that skill. The list went on—I was energized.

Second: "Be careful of your friends." Having entered a new school, I left most of my close friends behind, as they now attended another high school. Desperate to fit in, anyone who would eat lunch with me became a "friend." Even though these people were not the kind of people you would like to have "rub off" on you, I did not seem to be able to meet others. I made a commitment at camp to associate only with those people whose attitudes and morals fit were I wanted to go in life. I was clueless as to how hard this would be. Friendships like that are hard to find in high school, as most kids just want to fit in; but I was determined that only positive people were going to influence me.

Third: "Read stories of people who used what they had to become successful." Biographies became my "go to" read. The lives of presidents, entrepreneurs, explorers, and inventors filled my reading list from then on. I was inspired by their success and determined to use their examples at school to get ahead. I could see myself doing the same things they did.

Leaving camp that summer, I was motivated, inspired, and educated as to how to develop a positive self-image. I was on such a high that nothing could stop me. I still had a long way to go, I still had my shyness to overcome, I still needed to work on presenting myself in a positive manner, but I knew I was a work in progress. After all, "God don't make no junk!" It was only several weeks after camp that I noticed the references given for the material presented. "Adapted from See You at the Top, by Zig Ziglar." Funny name, but this guy must know his stuff—because it was working in me.

Many years later, as a high school agriculture teacher and FFA club adviser, I was very aware of the self-image problems my students were going through. I could see their potential, and I knew that they could do greater things than they ever realized, if they could only see themselves as I saw them—special and unique creations of God who have the potential to accomplish so much. I rediscovered the material from that camp 10 years earlier and integrated it into how I taught. The results were amazing. Shy, quiet girls became leaders of large clubs competing in leadership contests at state levels. Awkward, introverted boys led large group meetings and confidently spoke in front of audiences in our school community. All because they learned from me what I had learned as a freshman from FFA camp leaders who had been taught these principles from someone who had learned it directly from Zig Ziglar. That is exponential influence.

A goal properly set is halfway reached. —Zig Ziglar

My second Ziglar moment came during the summer following my junior year of high school. I had been chosen by my high school advisors to attend a leadership conference in Washington, D.C. The week was amazing—full of new friendships, new experiences, and a wealth of leadership training. One session that especially stuck with me was the goal-setting workshop. Since that first summer of camp, I had heard the importance of setting goals. However, this was different—or maybe I was just ready to hear it—as what was taught struck me as the most important lesson I had heard.

The workshop leaders started by identifying the roadblocks people had for not setting goals. The first one was fear, specifically fear of failure. That was me. I had long been afraid to set goals, and especially express them, because what if I failed? What would people say? I had never considered that fear of failing was so strong in me but, as the workshop progressed, I realized it had paralyzed me from trying new opportunities and reaching my potential. I still remember writing down in my notebook "No more fear." I was committing myself to moving forward—but how?

Luckily, the last roadblock was that people don't know how. The next hour was devoted to teaching the workshop participants the details of setting goals. The seven steps of goal-setting activity taught that day was revolutionary. I was fired up with this new information and could not wait to get back to my hotel room and start the process. I literally worked for three hours that evening examining each area of my life, setting goals for each of them, and then prioritizing them. The quote inside the goal-setting section of the workbook, "What you get by achieving your goals is not as important as what you become by achieving your goals," electrified me to work harder, as I was anxious to see all that I could accomplish and become.

Once back home, my first goal was to be the first at my high school to be accepted into college that fall. Even though I knew there would be many of my graduating class going to college, I wanted to be the first to receive an acceptance letter that fall. I would also be the first in my family to go to college as well, so motivation was not a problem. I carefully went step by step through the seven-step process, laying out the plan to accomplish this. The first week in October, 1986, a full month before anyone received theirs, and before most had even applied, I received my acceptance letter to North Carolina State University. As I looked over the leadership conference materials to see how this could help me in other areas, I noticed the reference for the goal-setting workshop: "adapted from Zig Ziglar material." All the steps, the roadblock information, and several of the quotes were Zig's—and I had no idea.

Later in college, I was privileged to have opportunities to teach this same seven-step goal-setting procedure to middle and high school students in ten different states. Thousands of students in these states learned these goal-setting principles from me, the same principles I had learned from workshop leaders, who in turn had learned from Ziglar. Ziglar had helped me be the first in my family to reach college, yet I had never met him in person or read any of his books. What an amazing influence!

> *You can have everything in life you want, if you will just help enough other people get what they want.* —Zig Ziglar

Once in college, I felt I was on a roll. With the knowledge of how to maintain a healthy self-image and successfully construct a goals program, alongside other leadership training I had been given, I was working and doing well in life. As state president of North Carolina's FFA association, I had reached one of my major goals. I thought the world was at my feet and that everyone would and should recognize the successful confident person I was. My "healthy self-image" was beginning to move toward becoming an arrogant ego. During a personal coaching session with Mickey McCall, a national FFA officer, he shared a quote he had heard at Zig Ziglar's "Born to Win" conference: "You can have everything in life you want, if you will just help enough other people get what they want." That sounded all good and everything, and made for a good slogan, but how did it affect me? I was too busy moving in the direction I wanted to worry about what others wanted. Yet I could not get that quote out of my head.

Months later, after failing to reach one of my goals, I took a long serious look at where I had come up short. I could not find anything wrong with my plan; it looked perfect to me. Then it hit me. My "why" for setting this goal and working toward it was all wrong. Everything about what I was trying to do and how I was going about it was clearly focused on me, and how it would benefit me. All the training I had had I was using with a "me first" approach, and I was beginning to see things fall apart. It was then that I remembered Ziglar's quote: "You can have everything you want, if you will just help enough other people get what they want." At first, I thought only of trying to discover what people wanted so I could move toward my goals. Then, I discovered the true, deeper meaning of this quote. True personal success comes as a by-product of helping others, not as the reason for helping others. I realized that if I just focused on helping others, using my God-given talents and gifts to enable others to succeed, I too would realize true success.

My whole approach to what I wanted to do with my life changed. Instead of trying to find opportunities to speak in front of large groups, I worked at a small Christian boy's camp serving the campers and staff in any way possible. Instead of vying for corporate jobs or even working in the family's nursery business, I elected to teach high school, opening up new programs in schools so I would have an opportunity to teach the personal development skills I had learned. The by-product was happiness, friends, peace of mind, health—and more opportunities to serve. All these, plus more, are what Ziglar identified 40 years ago as the foundation stones of a successful life. Ziglar was right! If you focus on your work, family life, faith life, with friends or in any area where you are helping others to achieve what they want in life, your success will be a natural by-product.

What an amazing philosophy! What a great way to lead your life! I wish I could say I have always remained true to that philosophy, but I have not. I believe for at least a decade I again shifted focus to my needs and desires at the expense of others. While still successful in the public's eye, I still lacked the sense of purpose I once felt. Then, the opportunity to partner with the Zig Ziglar corporation and become one of their founding Legacy trainers presented itself. I jumped at the opportunity, not knowing where it would lead or what the end result would be. I have no idea what the future holds, but I do know that I will use the lessons I've learned over my lifetime from Zig Ziglar to help others.

So how can someone whom you have never met, never spoken to, or never seen in person impact your life in such a dramatic way? Zig Ziglar did it by impacting people so much that they wanted to help others succeed. I am a product of his teaching and, if God provides me the opportunity, I will spend my time conveying his message of hope. ❧

JAMES McLAMB

Teacher, businessman, speaker, trainer, husband, father of three, athletic and fitness coach are all titles that describe James McLamb. James was an award-winning agriculture teacher in North Carolina before returning to the family-owned nursery to serve as president of a multi million-dollar company. Along the way he developed a love for coaching youth baseball and became a fitness coach to clients across the nation. His love for all things Ziglar started at a leadership camp his freshman year of high school; he has been hard core ever since. As one of the founding Ziglar Legacy Certified trainers, he is taking his years of varied experiences to help others "Be, Do, and Have" what they desire in life.

James McLamb
1312 Hedgelawn Way
Raleigh NC 27615
919-669-3971
www.jamesmclamb.com

LESSONS THROUGH ADVERSITY

By David Mineer

YOU CAN HAVE anything in life you want if you will just help enough other people get what they want" — Zig Ziglar. That, for me, is the most memorable quote from Zig Ziglar, and it solidifies for me the gospel principle of service that had been a regular part of my childhood as I attended church and learned from my parents inside our home.

When I was first starting my own family and my professional career, I was looking for help. By nature I was positive, energetic, and willing to work hard to fulfill my responsibility as a husband and father. But I wanted to be great. I had an insatiable appetite for learning and, although I was a horrible student at college, I really loved to hear the words of successful people who had been kind enough to share what they had learned with the world. It was during this time that I purchased some Zig Ziglar CD's to listen to in my car. I don't travel a lot but I do spend quite a bit of time on the road. That was the beginning of automobile university for me.

Over the years I have listened to literally hundreds, if not thousands, of different audio programs by a variety of authors. There is so much good information out there. And now, with the programs that make listening easy and the devices that can hold countless hours of quality information, we really do live in a golden age of information.

I am a result of this information and education. Zig explained it when he said: "You are what you are and you are where you are because of what has gone into your mind." The other half of that quote is "You change what you are and you change where you are by changing what goes into your mind." So, no matter where you are or where you have been, you can change. Life is full of so many ups and downs that it is important that we remember this.

I was raised in a good home with parents who loved me very much. I knew they loved me, and it provided a stability that will stay with me for my entire life. I hope that I have been as good a parent to my own children as my parents were to me. A love for my Savior Jesus Christ has always been a fundamental part of my life. I grew up attending church each week where we were taught the principles modeled by the one perfect person, Jesus Christ Himself. These principles include love, faith, hope, and service, along with many others. I was always taught to be kind to others, to treat them as you would like them to treat you.

As a young man growing up in the Church of Jesus Christ of Latter Day Saints, I always looked forward to serving a mission. That means giving two years of your life to sharing the gospel full-time. However, as a teenager who thought he knew everything, my dedication to this goal waivered, and I questioned whether or not I could leave so many things that I thought were important. Thankfully, the example of several of my friends and my mom's patient encouragement guided me back to where

I knew I wanted be.

I was called to serve in the Spanish Las Palmas (The Canary Islands) mission. I had no idea what a profound effect this opportunity would have on my life. For two years, my total life purpose was to serve the beautiful Spanish (Canarian) people sharing the gospel with those who would listen, and serving all of them. I made lifelong friends, testimonies were strengthened, and I grew closer to my Father in heaven as I diligently served. It is my hope that my entire life will be patterned after those two years when I served with all my heart, might, mind, and strength. My oldest daughter now serves, having been called to South Korea.

After returning home from serving in the Canary Islands, it was only four months later that I was watching one of my best friends get married. At his reception, on the other side of the line, was a beautiful woman whom I had never met. Who would have thought that as a groomsman I would see my future wife for the first time as a bridesmaid in my friend's wedding line? It happens, and it happened to me. A little over a year later, I married that sweet lady. She is the great blessing in my life. I am blessed to have such a beautiful, loving, caring wife.

My entire life revolves around my wife and our five beautiful children. Life has "special" moments that make us who are, and it is difficult to imagine our life void of these special times. Marriage is a big one. Choosing a spouse is such an important decision. I knew my wife was awesome when we were dating, but I could never have guessed or known how incredible she would be. Marriage—and life—bring many difficult challenges. At times, it can seem impossible. But those impossible moments remind us how special the "good times" are, and they remind us to never take for granted those precious moments that life has to offer.

Other special moments have been the births of my five children. I can't imagine my life without any of the five. They each fill a special place in my heart and in our family. I am constantly amazed how different they each are—born of the same parents, but each with unique personalities, skills, passions, and abilities. Each day, I marvel at how much I love them and how much they each bless my life.

I love my immediate and extended family. I believe family is the basic unit of society. I also believe, as David O. McKay states, that "No other success can compensate for failure in the home." It's that important that we give our best effort to be good, righteous, loving fathers and husbands. How can we be good fathers and husbands? I think a good guide can be found in *The Family, A Proclamation to the World*, where it states the following: "Successful marriages and families are established and maintained on principles of faith, prayer, repentance, forgiveness, respect, love, compassion, work, and wholesome recreational activities."

As we go about our daily lives, we become so busy and so caught up in the overwhelming task of providing for our families, spending time with our spouses and kids, and just trying to keep up, that we often overlook opportunities to serve others. We sometimes feel that it is too much for us to simply attend to our own matters. But then a miracle happens. We find that when we lose ourselves in the service of others we find such a sense of fulfillment, peace, and joy that we mysteriously find other aspects of our lives improving alongside this service.

Several years ago, I was taught a valuable lesson that I will never forget. It is customary for my family to vacation to Southern California every other year. We travel with a large group that consists of friends and families from my wife's clogging group. (Clogging is a type of power tap dancing.)

The day before we left, I had returned home from supervising a youth, three-day camp out. There was nothing out of the ordinary about this camp, although when I got home I was sick that evening, which was the evening before we were heading to Southern California. At the camp, as usually happens, the mosquitoes were everywhere, and I had been bitten a bunch of times. Particularly interesting was a triangle pattern of three mosquito bites on my knee. This wasn't a big deal, and so I didn't give it a second thought.

By the time we left on the charter bus for our vacation I felt much better. We stopped in Las Vegas about three hours into the journey, and everything was great. We were so excited to be going on vacation. The kids were talking about the fun they would have at Disneyland, the beach, Knots Berry Farm, and other locations we knew we would be visiting.

A highlight of any trip to Southern California is a stop in Barstow at the In-N-Out Burger. I'm not sure why, but I absolutely love to eat there. As we exited the bus, I noticed my knee was stiff and even hurt a little bit. This isn't completely unheard of, as I am tall; being crammed on a bus, or especially an airplane, is often devastating to my knees. So we continued and ordered our food. About half-way through my meal I could eat no more. The pain in my knee had become such that I couldn't finish one of my favorite meals in the whole world. If nothing else, this fact alone was an indication of a serious problem. We boarded the bus and continued on to Anaheim. This was the most uncomfortable bus ride I ever took. Nothing I did helped to relieve the pain I was experiencing in my knee. It was not a pleasant ride. Arriving at the hotel, I could barely move. Even the good parts of my body were hard to move because every movement caused severe pain in that bad knee.

I am usually one to jump off the bus and help everyone with their lug-
gage. Not this time.

After getting my family situated in the hotel room, I took a cab to the
nearest emergency room. I was so distraught that already I was ruining
what we expected to be a perfect family vacation. By this time, I could
barely walk, and as I entered the emergency room the nurse noticed
that I was struggling. She asked me what my pain level was, from one to
10. I didn't have any history of injury, but I was in so much pain that
I explained, "I think it's gotta be somewhere in the range of a 10." But
not wanting to be a baby, I told her, "Write down eight, I guess."

It wasn't too long before I was seen by a doctor. He shoved a needle
in my knee and gave me something that relieved the pain for the first
time in over eight hours. I felt so relieved. The doctor wasn't sure what
was causing my pain, and I think they wondered if I was exaggerating
the amount of pain I felt. Not knowing exactly what was wrong with
me, they diagnosed it as gout and gave me some medication for that,
and some for the pain, and sent me away. I called another cab to take
me to the nearest pharmacy for the medication and then another cab to
get me back to the hotel.

Those of you who have vacationed with young families may understand this, but having to pay several cab fares was forcing me to use
money that I didn't have a lot of and that I needed for the family vacation.

I made it back to the hotel later that night after the family was asleep
in the room. I got into bed and tried to sleep. I slept only a little, and
finally at about 4:00 a.m. I was up for good. I went around to the front
of the hotel so I wouldn't interrupt my family and could figure out what
else I could do for this mysterious, horrible pain that I was having in my
knee. I found the nearest office of an orthopedic specialist. But it didn't

open until 9:00 a.m. So, with several hours to go and not feeling like I could afford more cab rides I planned a route that would allow me to take buses to that doctor's office. It actually looked good because it was just two buses, with one bus-to-bus transfer.

At the appropriate time, I set out from the hotel on my crutches in severe pain. It had rained lightly and was actually still raining when I left. This made it slippery for my crutches, and in my attempts to protect that knee from moving, the crutch would slip and the pain would be unbearable. I remember several people asking if I needed assistance. I had only about a half-block to go from the hotel to the bus stop. The bus driver, seeing my struggle to get to the bus and into a seat, only charged me the discounted handicapped rate. This was when I first considered what it was like to be handicapped.

I boarded that bus and after a few short blocks we were to my first stop. I exited the bus and stood on the side to survey what I needed to do next. I only had to go back about 40 yards to the light, cross the street, and go another 40 yards to the next bus stop where I would continue in the other direction. At this moment, I was graciously taught a valuable lesson that I will never forget. I learned that there are things that I had taken for granted. Normally, I would have raced across that street, probably not even in the crosswalk, and been over to that next bus stop in a matter of seconds—and that's if I would have even taken the bus, because normally I could have easily walked several blocks, or even miles. Not this time. Getting that short distance to that next bus stop was excruciating. Not only was the pain immense but physically I wasn't sure I would be able to make it.

I had gone from playing basketball three days a week to barely being able to move. Each movement brought with it unbearable pain. As I have reflected on this and my following recovery period, I have come to appreciate the accommodations for those who are handicapped. For the next month, I would come to depend on that extra little help that those accommodations provided. There were times when if there wasn't a handicapped spot near the building I needed to enter I wouldn't go in there because I worried I would not have the strength to make it in, complete my errand, and get back to the car. Handicapped spots had previously been a source of frustration to me because they were often the only spaces available, and it seemed they didn't get used. But now I understood why it was so very important that they were available to those who need them.

I got to the doctor's office about a half-hour early and waited patiently. It turned out that this particular office did not open that day, and so this difficult trip had been completely in vain. Once I realized this, I crossed the street in a hurry to catch a bus which I had seen. I nearly fell in the middle of the street, and I remember thinking I wasn't sure if I could get myself back up if I did. I did not fall, and I got onto the bus. Many good people noticed I wasn't all right and offered assistance. As I boarded the bus and sat in a handicapped seat I could not bend my hurt knee, and being tall, 6'6", my leg stuck out and blocked almost the entire aisle. This was at the front of the bus. Many seemed understanding, but several obviously considered it rude that I would leave my leg sticking out there. A lesson my father taught me is to always give people the benefit of the doubt. If you have to step over somebody's leg, maybe it's because they can't physically bend it to get it out of your way.

I made it back to the hotel and rented a car to take me to a hospital that had an orthopedic surgeon. They took a look at me and took what they needed to run some tests, and they sent me away with some different medications. Leaving that office in the rental car and heading to the pharmacy was the next moment when I began to feel hopeless. The doctor wasn't sure what was up, and I was in excruciating pain. I began to wonder if I would ever again be able to do some of the things that I enjoy. I love sports and the outdoors. All of a sudden, it looked as if I might never be able to do some of those things again, especially not at a hundred percent.

The next day I rented a "jazzy" so I could at least try and hang out with the family at Disneyland. It worked well, and it did get me around. The pain medication helped with the pain, and while it wasn't a great day, I was happy to be able to enjoy the time with my family as they enjoyed the "Happiest Place on Earth."

After a few calls to the doctor that evening we finally got the results of the tests and it turned out that I had a "strep" infection in my knee. The doctor recommended that I return home as soon as possible and have a local orthopedic surgeon operate on my knee. We quickly made flight arrangements. The only problem was, we don't live near a major airport so it took some planning to get me home. My wife and I agreed that they wouldn't be able to do anything at home so my family would stay and try to finish the vacation and hopefully enjoy the time, even though I wouldn't be there.

I got a ride from friends to the Orange County Airport. I struggled into the airport late, and worried I wouldn't make that last flight of the evening to Las Vegas. To my dismay, my gate was the furthest away. One of the security people asked if I needed assistance and, since I was in such a hurry and thought for sure that would make me miss the flight, I declined. I struggled to the gate to catch my flight. I made it and took my seat. By this time I was exhausted and the medication was starting to cause nightmares—like horror movie nightmares. During the short one-hour flight to Vegas I kept jumpin' in my seat as I drifted in and out of sleep and was awoken by stupid nightmares.

Arriving in Las Vegas, I again ended up at an area that couldn't have been further away from the pickup area where my brother-in-law was waiting for me. As I struggled to make it through the airport, I asked several airport employees if I could get any assistance, like a golf cart to pick me up. They were kind but told me that since I hadn't requested that assistance when boarding the flight at the point of departure they wouldn't be able to get anyone, at least not quickly.

About that time, the handle on one of my crutches broke. This was, up to now, the low point in my life. I honestly thought that there was a real possibility that I would fall unconscious to the floor and die right there in the Las Vegas airport. I couldn't imagine that I would be able to make it to the pickup area where I had a ride waiting for me. I thought that might be the end. But, I was so determined to make it that I don't remember thinking about much other than I just had to make it.

I did make it. The next morning they operated and removed as much of the infection as they could. I spent the next 30 days in IV therapy with a picc line (a form of catheter) to administer antibiotics. I was in a lot of pain, especially the first two weeks, and almost totally dependent on my wife during my recovery.

It's often an experience like this that makes you step back and appreciate life. I feel I have always had gratitude in my heart for the many blessings in my life. But now I take less for granted and I try harder to help those who need my help.

I have recovered 100 percent from the effects of this infection. They are not even sure what caused it. They speculate that possibly the mosquito bites allowed the infection access to my knee, where it was able to thrive and cause me the pain that it did.

I pray that this experience will remind me of the important things in life: That I will search out opportunities to help and serve others; that my efforts might bring happiness and at least a moment of relief to anyone who is suffering.

It's in our service to others that we will find happiness. We can make a difference in our own lives and in the lives of others. I believe Zig Ziglar when he said, "You were designed for accomplishment, engineered for success, and endowed with the seeds of greatness!" ∽

DAVID MINEER

David Mineer is the CEO of Construction Monitor, a company that his father founded in 1989 to help businesses succeed by providing targeted information. He helped Construction Monitor grow from providing hundreds of building permit leads in a single state to over 17,000 each week from 65 areas across the United States. David never misses early morning basketball and while earning his bachelor degree in Business Administration from Southern Utah University, he walked onto the baseball team and helped them to a record of 6 – 54 (yes, 6 wins and 54 losses). He is married to Heather and has five kids.

David Mineer
Construction Monitor
P.O. BOX 2202
Cedar City, UT 84720
mineerjr@constructionmonitor.com
435-590-1205

IT'S ONLY HARD 'TIL YOU LEARN IT

By Michael Ray Newman

WANT TO KNOW the cruel thing about dyslexia? The way it's spelled: "Dyslexia."

Seriously, how are you going to give a name like that to a condition about having trouble stringing letters and words together?

If you want someone with dyslexia to be able to explain their condition with the written word, you name it something simple, like "Dis." Three letters. Not complicated.

Or at least you spell it with easier-to-remember letters—maybe something like "dislecksia" (emphasis on the "dis" because that's what it does—it disses you).

But that's the thing about spelling the word—it came to define my school days. It's just like everything else in life that's difficult to master: It's only hard till you learn it.

The reason I bring up dyslexia here is because the moral of this chapter reminds me of a couple of stories from my life that really opened my eyes to the kind of hard work it takes to be successful in business (and as a parent, for that matter).

When I was a kid, I couldn't spell. Unfortunately, at my school, just because you couldn't do something didn't mean they were going to let you off the hook.

Back in third grade, when I was first learning how to spell complex words, our teacher would give us a new set of words every Monday. There were only ten words each week, but we'd have to learn them in time for the spelling tests every Friday, and spelling words wasn't exactly my specialty at the time.

As a kid with undiagnosed dyslexia, spelling was just about enough to give me a coronary every week. I would dread the process so much that I would always put off learning the words until Thursday night. Then, like clockwork, every Thursday my dad would come to me and give me a little kick in the pants about the homework.

"Time to start your spellin'," he'd say in his Texas drawl. "Get in your room and learn those words."

My dad had good grades in school, so I think that's why he would get so frustrated with my struggles. Either way, it didn't take me too long to learn not to cross him on spelling.

So I'd trot off to my room for an hour or so, looking over those ten words, again and again. I'd spell them in my mind, spell them out loud, spell them in different orders, try to use them in a sentence (writing each sentence down five times over)—anything I could do to make them stick.

Between my dyslexia and my anxiety over the task of having to learn something that was next to impossible for me to learn, the knowledge I'd just drilled into my head for an hour would always be gone by the time I returned to the living room to demonstrate to my dad what I'd learned.

"Spell 'eligible,'" he would say.

"Eligible..." I would pause, feeling a cold sweat coming to my brow. I had just spelled the word out loud about thirty times in my room. I'd seen the word again and again and again. I'd spoken it, written it, repeated it so many times I got bored repeating it. But the moment my dad asked me to spell it, I froze up.

"No, no," Dad interrupted. "Not two L's—one L."

I would clench my jaw, feeling helpless and afraid and frustrated with myself for disappointing my dad. So I would try again. And I felt as if I would always fail.

"How can you not spell 'eligible'?" Dad would ask, rising from his recliner to lead me into the kitchen. There, we would set up at the table so we could work on the words together. But by the time we sat down, I'd already be ready to cry.

It's not that Dad was too hard on me—it's just that he believed so highly that I could do it. And since we didn't know I had dyslexia, or even what dyslexia was for that matter, there was no way for him to understand that it wasn't lack of effort that was preventing me from learning the words.

The thing I remember most about these sessions with my father was sitting at that table with my hands pressed to my face so I could hide my tears from him. I never wanted Dad to see me cry.

Before my son Trent was diagnosed with dyslexia, I found myself doing the same thing to him.

At the time, we had him and his sister Presley both enrolled in this fancy private school. The place was so expensive (and I was so broke, trying to make my business work) that I was late with the tuition every semester. I was practically homeless and driving a beat-up old truck, but we always managed to make that school work in the budget. I don't ever remember paying tuition on time, but we always managed to get it paid.

Funny story about that truck: This was a rich, rich school, and there I was driving this old leaky, smoking, blue Chevy truck to drop off and pick up the kids. It only took the administration two weeks to ask me not to pull the thing up to the front of the school because I was leaving oil stains on the driveway.

Anyway, Trent was in second grade when the principal—the same guy who delivered the request for me to stop driving my truck on school property, and the same guy who used to hand me the late notices for my tuition checks—called my wife Carrie and me into his office to have a little chat about our son.

"This is a college preparatory school," he began.

"That's why we pay you the big money," I quipped.

He continued unfazed. "I just don't think your son has what it takes to succeed here."

My heart sank. I looked over at Carrie who wore no expression on her face.

"What do you mean?" she asked.

"Well," the principal said, hemming and hawing, "given his grades, we just think he would do better in a public school, where they have... *special* programs for...*special needs* children."

The way he accentuated the words "special needs," it was all I could do to keep from leaping over his desk and knocking him to the floor. "Are you calling my kid retarded?" I wanted to scream. Instead, I seethed, letting the haughty principal have his say about why and why not my son could hack it at his overpriced grade school. I couldn't shake the idea that he was insulting my son.

Strangely, at the same time, it was all kind of a load off for me because I knew it meant I wouldn't have to pay two tuitions at this place anymore.

When we left that awful meeting, Carrie and I had a long talk about what we were going to do.

We knew our son was smart, but his grades didn't seem to reflect that fact. More and more, it seemed to us that he might have dyslexia.

By then, were both well aware of the effects of dyslexia because my younger brother had been diagnosed with a severe case, and so had Carrie's brother. With that in mind, I went to my mom with the story of our meeting with the principal.

"Yeah, I'd say it sounds like dyslexia," she said. Then she brightened up. "You should take him to Miss Martin." Helen Martin is a world-renowned expert on dyslexia. As it happened, she lived in the same neighborhood I did in the Dallas–Fort Worth area and had already diagnosed and tutored my brother and Carrie's brother through their struggles with the condition.

The idea that we would have to take our son to a dyslexia specialist really floored me. When I heard my mother's opinion on the matter, I could hardly take it. It's like a parent's worst nightmare—the idea that they passed off one of their worst qualities to their child.

The whole thing got me thinking about my memories of working on my homework with my dad.

Most of the time, Carrie would help Trent with his homework because I would just get too frustrated because of my own insecurities about school. I just saw so much of myself in him whenever he struggled.

Up to that point, I thought I had been doing it differently than my dad had done with me because I wouldn't send him off to his room on his own first to learn things such as his spelling words. Instead, Carrie (or, in some situations, I) would always sit down with him at the table to learn them together.

But you know that old yarn about how we become our parents? Well, in this case, it was true. It didn't occur to me how hard I was pushing Trent until I saw a big old crocodile tear fall right onto his paper. It splashed down right onto spelling word number two. Those pains you struggled with growing up hurt far worse when you have to watch them in your children.

Most of the time, even when I was on homework duty, I'd get too frustrated and would have to remove myself from the room so Carrie could finish in my place. I just never wanted to berate my son for his difficulty at grasping his homework. But now that the difficulty had become apparent to the administrators at his school, it felt like the time was right to visit the specialist.

"From what you are telling me," Miss Martin said, "it sounds like he is dyslexic."

Of course, we'd had a feeling all along that it was dyslexia, but still, it was a shock to hear it spoken aloud. And given the fact that I saw so much of myself in my son, it felt almost like I was finally getting a diagnosis for myself at the same time.

"How can we be sure?" I asked Miss Martin.

She furrowed her brow. "Well, what does he do for fun? Does he play any sports?"

"As a matter of fact, he has a hockey game right down the street from your house on Saturday."

"That's what I'll do then. I'll come to see him play."

So Miss Martin came out to watch Trent play his favorite sport. My son has always been pretty good at hockey. He has an incredible skill to play the angles and see how the game is going to unfold before anyone else on the ice. On that day, he dominated the competition.

Miss Martin picked up on that immediately.

It's clear from the way he plays that he's very smart," she said. "Most likely, it's just dyslexia. We'll need to get him tested to see exactly what we're dealing with."

When the tests came back, we found that our son's IQ was excellent. But, yes, he did have dyslexia.

The day I learned for certain that my son suffered from the same condition that had plagued me all my life, I came to two realizations. First, I was going to do everything in my power to help Trent manage his dyslexia in a more positive way than I had managed mine.

For me, dyslexia was an unnamed fear—that icy thing that gripped my mind whenever I had to learn a spelling word and seized my throat whenever I had to read aloud in class. Dyslexia would drive me to make excuses and avoid homework. It would drive me to sit in the back of every class. It taught me the fine art of cheating to get by.

Trent would embrace the condition, owning it as something he merely has to deal with. He wouldn't hide his dyslexia. He would use it to propel him to get better every day. He would always sit in the front of the class, and he would always explain himself if he had trouble mastering an assignment.

The second realization I had that day was this: "It's only hard 'til you learn it." Almost nothing worth having in life comes easy.

After hearing about the diagnosis, Trent asked me what it meant. I never acted like it was a big deal or that he was different or lesser than anyone else. I just said, "All it means is that it's only hard 'til you learn it. You're just going to have to work harder at it than other people."

"Think about the first time you tried to skate," I told him. "Or the first time you tried hitting a baseball. That didn't come easy at first, did it?"

Trent shook his head.

"But now what? Now you're great at both of those things. And it's all because you worked hard to learn them."

The same is true for literally everything in life that is difficult at first. It's only hard 'til you learn it. Then it becomes easier, and eventually it becomes like second nature.

From that day forward, whenever Trent struggled with something, I would remind him of the tools Miss Martin had provided to help him succeed. And if he thought something was too difficult, I would always remind him of the lesson about hard work and about using the strategies he had been taught to overcome his difficulties.

Whenever he got really down about his struggles, I would try to pick him up with little reminders about his strengths. "A lot of things come easy to you," I would say. "You're a good athlete. All you have to do with this is to learn it differently than everybody else.

Some days, it didn't matter—the struggles would continue regardless. On those days, I would remind him of when he first began playing hockey. He's always had natural ability with the sport. That first year, he was head and shoulders better than the other kids. He was so good and so fast that sometimes he would fall down a bunch of times whenever they did their drills.

"You did great, Bud," I said to him after one such practice.

"But I kept falling down," he told me, clearly disappointed with himself even though he skated circles around everyone.

"If you don't fall down, you'll never get any better."

He looked at me funny. "What do you mean?"

"If you always stay in your comfort zone, you'll never get any better. You've got to keep pushing your edges if you want to improve."

Sometimes I still overhear Trent sharing this wisdom with others. "If you don't fall, you're not getter any better," he once said to Lily, our youngest. But that's the truth about anything in life. It's only hard 'til you learn it. And if you don't fall, you'll never get any better.

My business career is proof of both. Nothing came easy to me at first. And if there's an entrepreneur out there who's fallen more times than I have, I'd sure like to meet him. Not knowing about and owning my dyslexia caused my life to take shape in a much different way than Trent's.

I learned how to cheat my way into college and wound up dropping out. Trent learned to manage his condition by using the strategies he was taught, and he wound up being a two-sport college athlete with a 3.56 GPA.

Conclusion

As Zig Ziglar said: "You were designed for accomplishment, engineered for success, and empowered with the seeds of greatness."

The first time I heard this quote was in my early 20's while going from garage sale to yard sale looking for baby clothes for my first-born, Presley Elise. I had bought a handful of cassette tapes for a buck twenty five and one was about sales and this quote was in it...Mr. Ziglar repeated that quote over and over to me the next few months until my cassette player ate the tape.

And it's been something I have instilled in all of my children from the day they were born. I had always had the seeds of greatness in me, I just needed to learn a different way of growing them.

I am grateful for my dyslexia.

I have learned how to take my disability and turn it into an ability. My dyslexia has allowed me to develop a methodology that gives me a unique way of looking at problems and turning those problems into opportunities and solutions. We have all been endowed with seeds of greatness. It's up to us to learn how to cultivate nature and grow those seeds. It's also imperative we help our children realize their potential and SHOW them how to cultivate the greatness within themselves.

The ability of my disability. ❧

MICHAEL RAY NEWMAN

Michael Ray's energetic and enthusiastic approach to all areas of his life best defines how he handles tasks as a professional speaker, trainer, inventor, consultant, and successful entrepreneur.

Michael's success in leadership comes from his lifestyle philosophy "WHATEVER IT TAKES (W.I.T.)." Michael leads by example as well as action, not simply by empty lip service.

His modest upbringing started at the bottom and has led to the prestigious positions he holds today, making it easy for him to relate to corporate businessmen and women and entrepreneurs alike. With a challenging learning disability and his background in the business world, Michael Ray has established himself as a true inspiration to others. His relentless pursuit of running smarter, more efficient operations, along with his out-of-the-box ideology and turning those ideas into multi-million dollar companies, has put him on the map as a prominent entrepreneur.

Michael's belief is that if you have a well-thought-out plan and you are committed to do whatever it takes, then you will succeed! And success breeds confidence. This in turn encircles us with a positive "can do" attitude that not only helps our business, but our personal relationships as well. This fearless "never give up" attitude coupled with his enthusiastic and motivational approach is the reason that Michael Ray has become one of the most sought-after consultants, trainers, and keynote speakers today.

Michael Ray Newman
214-695-0960

THE COACH AND CLASS THAT CHANGED THE TRAJECTORY OF MY LIFE

By Rick R Richards

I WAS UP to bat against one of our biggest rivals in the area. Canyon High School. The pitch came in, and I drove a sharp line drive over the second baseman's head, into the gap in right center field. As I rounded first, my base coach teammate was yelling, "Go two...Go two!!" I glanced up and saw that the ball was in between the two outfielders and I felt I had a good chance to make it to second. I dove head first into the bag for my first double of my senior year varsity season. I ended up scoring during that inning and felt great about contributing, helping my team win the game against a very formidable opponent.

Reflecting on that moment, I had just achieved something in real life that I had only imagined myself accomplishing just a few weeks before. It was then I realized that the course I had been studying in school, a course called "Strategy" led by my baseball coach, was going to impact me and change the path of my life forever.

It was 1980, and I was a senior at Saugus High School, located in the Santa Clarita Valley of sunny Southern California, some thirty miles north of Hollywood. Canyon High School, our opposition that day, was located only five miles from our campus and always was a very imposing team to beat.

I was a true die-hard baseball player. From T-ball as a young boy through my late teens, I was smitten. In high school, I played two years with the junior varsity, and my last two years with the varsity squad. I tried out for the basketball teams and didn't make the cuts, and never attempted football, largely with the advice of my Dad who did not want me to end up like my uncle Tom. He was burdened with bad knees throughout his life as a result of football injuries incurred as a young man.

Baseball was my sport. Even as I entered my post high school academics, I tried out for the baseball team at College of the Canyons Junior College, coached by a successful manager, Mike Gillespie. I came up a bit short in that pursuit, which brought a close to my competitive baseball career.

But that double in the Canyon High game was a very special one for me. I was not on the first string at the time, and since my designated position was shortstop, there were times that I only played a portion of a game, and times I never played at all. I knew my role. I was, however, gifted with sound hitting skills, able to make contact and drive the ball to all fields.

Doug Worley, my attentive and instructive head coach, was aware of my strengths and weaknesses. For this particular game, he put me in the starting lineup in right field, knowing that my bat might be needed in this game. I was excited to play and eager to do my very best. I truly will never forget that game or opportunity.

I called and talked with Coach Worley before I wrote this chapter to receive his permission to mention him in this publication. I had not spoken to him in over 15 years, and the last time I had seen him was at my twenty year high school reunion. In our lengthy phone conversation, we spoke about many things. We shared our experiences about life, family, faith and baseball.

I even asked Coach Worley if he recalled that game against Canyon High some thirty plus years ago. Much to my surprise, he said he did. It was not for my line drive double, but for a defensive play I had made in right field. I had run down a fly ball to right, dove to make the catch, and had the umpire end up seeing it differently. The ump said I had trapped the ball, and gave the batter a base hit. Coach and I are still convinced to this day that I made that catch. All in all, we were both happy at the effort I put in on that day.

That game proved to be the pinnacle of what I had been working on so very hard over the prior few months. Before the start of the baseball season, Coach Worley had suggested that all of the baseball players enroll into a new class he was teaching called "Strategy". The choice to attend this new course was easy, mostly because it was going to be taught by our baseball coach, and the whole team would be participating in taking one of the classes offered.

The outline of the course was set out and the textbook was called "See You at the Top", authored by Zig Ziglar. I had no idea who Zig Ziglar was, and as with all of my peers, we just thought he had a funny name. This book was a newly published book at the time and Mr. Ziglar was just beginning to have an affect on our society and his influence was changing lives of people, dramatically, one at a time.

This class was about building a better self image, building winning relationships with other people and developing a goal-setting program to help you achieve everything you wanted to get out of life. Zig Ziglar's book was full of wonderful stories that would impact the reader in a deep, profound way. These stories would cause your thinking to change and then, if you were willing to apply the principles, your behavior would change for the better. This class should be required in every high school across the United States. We would be graduating thousands of high school seniors who would have the needed skills to become a success in life. Having the right positive mental attitude towards life is the key.

Certainly, one of the most powerful principles I learned from my coach through that class can be summed up in this one Ziglar quote. "You cannot perform in a manner inconsistent with the way you see yourself."

The reason I was able to play in that game and execute as I did, to make that catch, to connect with that double, was because of the truth in that quote. I knew that if I applied such exactness to my thinking and acted upon that, I would be able to perform.

During our baseball season, and because of our geographical location, there were times that we would be scheduled to play against schools that were 30 to 50 miles away from our campus. We would ride on the team bus to these other schools many times during the season. A few weeks before that game against Canyon High School mentioned earlier, we were scheduled to play Antelope Valley High, some 45 minutes away. With that lengthy bus ride, we had time to rest, think, talk and strategize about our game plan.

On the return ride home from that game, Coach Worley approached me and asked me if he could talk with me about a few things. Of course, I was all ears. He asked me to start imagining myself becoming more successful at hitting the baseball when up at bat. He asked me to start to develop a new belief system as to how I saw myself. He wanted me to see myself winning at baseball; from hitting effective line drives, to stopping ground balls, and to throwing accurately to teammates. He wanted me to imagine myself as a winner and not a loser. He was aware of my low self-image and turned his focus to helping me change my stinkin' thinkin.'

His encouragement that day impacted me in a profound way. The conversation, I'm sure, lasted only five minutes or so, but as I write this, I feel like time slowed down to almost a stop. Coach Worley's words to me could not have come at a better time in my life. I believe that God set up that time just for me in order to inject some hope for my future. My coach knew that I needed to see myself doing such a change in my mind first, before I could actually execute anything in real life. As Zig Ziglar teaches: "You have to plan to win, prepare to win, and then and only then can you expect to win."

This great change in my life almost didn't happen. I almost missed the opportunity to meet Coach Worley, play baseball, take the "Strategy" class, and become familiar with the books of Zig Ziglar if I didn't end up attending Saugus High School. I was born in Santa Monica, California, miles and miles from Saugus High School, and no way destined to attend that school.

But as our family grew in size with my parents having more children, we moved inland from Santa Monica to the San Fernando Valley, residing in a home in Granada Hills for a few years. With child number five on the way, my folks moved further inland, settling into a new and developing community in the Santa Clarita Valley called Newhall. Our growing family was now established, with Mom and Dad (Shirley and Bob) as our loving parents, three sisters (Kim, Jan, and Kristyn), myself, and my brother John. Kim, Jan and I were all born just one year apart, Kristyn is two years younger than I, and John is four years younger than I am.

As an aside, when the five of us kids were grown and out of the house, Mom and Dad became foster parents and fell in love with one of their foster children, who they adopted. His name is Patrick and he instantly became our 'youngest' brother. Patrick is 30 years younger than me.

I mention all my family members and their birth order so you can see we were all fairly close to each other in age, excepting Patrick. I felt most secure in this family unit and close to all my siblings. We all attended the same elementary school and the same junior high school. When we reached the age of high school, there were a number of issues that came to light involving changes in the school district policies.

In late 1976, the William S. Hart School District (named after the Hollywood western film legend who lived in the Newhall area in those earlier years) moved to institute busing in our neighborhoods, in an attempt to fill the attendance shortfalls in the newer built schools in the district. Our family members, as well as the kids in the neighborhood we lived in, were all planning on attending the high school that was more local to us instead of one that was much further away. Many of us in that age group were upset at this decision, and worried that we would be separated from our long-standing relationships.

When I entered Saugus High School as a freshman, I was terrified. I felt more than a little insecure in attending a new school, where I knew almost no one. I had that very low self-image, my confidence was dwindling, and leaving the security of being around my two older sisters didn't help. Even some of the friends I hung out with from my neighborhood didn't help.

My friends' comments and name calling were not at all kind, and even with me asking them to stop with the negative comments, I found myself yielding to their nonsense and start believing what they were saying. I never really seemed to perform well in school, working hard to maintain a "C" average throughout junior and senior high. The only classes in which I got "A's" were Physical Education and shop classes.

As a freshman in between classes, during lunch break, or as I walked to my locker I was always on edge. I thought that the "upper graders" (that is the term I used to describe sophomores and juniors) were going to "scrub" me, which was a humiliating ritual that underclassmen were exposed to that usually included getting beaten up and tossed into a trash can, head first. Fortunately for me, this never happened. I was living in fear of what might happen.

I mentioned sophomores and juniors in the preceding text for this reason. Being that Saugus was a brand new school, the classes were not full enough to have a senior class, so during the first year of high school, there were only freshmen, sophomores, and juniors. As the population in the surrounding communities grew, so did our campus. Looking back now, I am glad that the changes that took place in the school districts enabled me to attend Saugus High School. My self-image was ready for a complete makeover, and the convergence of classes, teachers, coaches, and sports gave me my first check-up from the neck up.

The program I discuss was that of the introduction of the "Strategy" class to our school in which I enrolled in 1979. It was an experimental pilot program that Coach Worley and his boss, Mr. Murdock, put together and wanted to test out on our campus. During that time, it was difficult to start up new and experimental classes of this nature, and it was certainly a brave move on their parts.

I believe God knew I needed to meet Coach Doug Worley and play baseball for him, but more importantly, that I was destined to take the newly formed "Strategy" class to learn of the principles Zig Ziglar taught. With all the changes in my life at that time; new schools, new friends, and the new high school environment, it was not apparent that the benefits of such a class were finding results right away. Little do we know that when we feel the direction of our life is going the wrong way, the seeds of success—the "Strategy" course—are taking root.

To this day, I will be forever grateful for these two forward-thinking teachers who took a risk that brought great results to countless students. Years and decades later, the successes of hundreds of Saugus High School students can be traced to those educators' efforts. I can honestly say that this class changed the course of my life. Go Centurions!

More about the awesome class that changed the trajectory of my life. The school named the class "Strategy" which is an appropriate name for the material we are covering. One of the meanings of the word 'strategy' is to "have a high-level plan to achieve one or more goals under conditions of uncertainty." Strategy is important because the resources available to achieve one's goals are usually limited. Strategy generally involves setting goals, determining actions to achieve the goals, and mobilizing resources to execute the actions. A strategy describes how the ends will be achieved by the means.

The text of Zig Ziglar's "See You At The Top" was first published in 1975, and it was based on Ziglar's first book called "Biscuits, Fleas, and Pump Handles" published in 1974.

As I dove into this class and into the book, hope arose inside of me. I learned that Mr. Ziglar was not a high-performing student in school and it was helpful for me to know that such a successful man in his life did not excel academically. That helped me connect with him in a strong way.

Zig Ziglar's honest admission that he was just an average guy, with no remarkable talents, gave me hope that I could become successful in my own right. He would say, "My wife was ranked fourth in a high school class of three hundred. I was part of the class that made the top half possible!" That was always a point that made me laugh but also convinced me that I could do something with my life as well.

Another of Mr. Ziglar's statements rang true to me. "Whatever success I have enjoyed as a speaker and author was not the result of some natural talent. My success was the result of hard work and practice." This quote motivated me in a great way and illustrated that hard work and consistent practice would produce great successes. This formula will produce success for anyone who will apply it. I have to thank Mr. Ziglar for introducing these principles into my life at the young age of 17.

I was never the best reader and reading books was always difficult for me. There was only one book I read on a regular basis and that was the Bible, but even then, to sit and read it was a struggle. My Dad purchased the Bible that was recorded on cassette tapes, which gave me the opportunity to follow along in the Bible (Good News For Modern Man edition) while listening to the tapes. Back in the 1970's, it was uncommon to have cassette tapes containing the Bible scriptures, but Dad found those that were made for the American Foundation for the Blind.

Often, I would come home from school, enter my parent's bedroom, and lie on their big bed. I would load up the cassette player and put on the Gospel of John and start to listen to the words and hear the start of each tape. The voice is still familiar in my mind. "Read by Bud Collier. Cassette one, track one, John, Chapter 1 through Chapter 6." And the voice would continue, reading scripture as I followed along in the text. Many times I would put down the Bible and just lay still and listen. Sometimes I would fall asleep, but every day that I did that, I knew that the truth of God's word was going into my mind and then I let it get down into my heart.

"See You at the Top" was the other book that sparked my interest. I wanted to read every chapter, and it was unusual for me to want to read so much. This book was indeed different. I wasn't really sure why at first, but as I kept reading the stories in each chapter, I was beginning to hear something very new that applied to me. I began to understand that I was valuable, that I had something to offer others, that I could accomplish something with my life if I decided to take action. The Ziglar messages were starting to take root inside of me. I didn't really know who I was or where I was going before I took this "Strategy" class. In the years leading up to this time in my life, I began to notice that a few of my childhood friends were making poor choices with their lives. Witnessing that, I decided to separate myself from them and not be tempted to participate, via peer pressure, in those destructive behaviors. This left me in a place where I would need to make new friends or just be a "loner" for a while until I was able to find new friends and outlets.

In high school, two things were most important to me. My walk with Jesus and baseball. As I mentioned earlier, I loved baseball from an early age, with my Dad starting me in T-ball and little league as soon as I was old enough to swing a bat. That affection for baseball was a constant in my youth and, as I noted, up and through high school.

My Christian walk also followed that same yearning. Following the lead of my parents, our family began attending a wonderful church in Van Nuys, California. "The Church on the Way" was led by Pastor Jack Hayford, it started out as a small church and grew by faith into a congregation of over 10,000. By coincidence or by guidance, "The Church on the Way" was actually situated on a street called "Sherman Way." Maybe it was the street name that became part of the legacy, or it may well be the fact that the attendees were "on their way" to becoming better people and stronger Christians. In any event, even though I do not live or attend there these days, it is still close to my heart.

Since I did not want to connect with friends anymore at my high school, those I felt were heading in a wrong direction, I really poured myself into my new friends at church. One of my lifelong friends from that time is Curtis Hanna. To this day, I connect with him on a weekly basis, and still call him my best friend. Our acquaintance began at our church youth group, attending summer and winter camps as well as church functions. We went to the beach, played pick-up football with church friends, and went to Christian concerts together. But best of all, Curtis loved Jesus with all of his heart, and that was the kind of friend I wanted to hang around with.

Curtis was always positive and encouraging to me. We shared many common interests, and snow skiing was among our favorites. He is one individual who I know truly loves me, who is willing to get into my face when needed, who asks the hard questions, and who demands accountability which enables me to grow as a person. Curtis is a great man of God, and I thank our Savior for allowing me the honor of calling him my friend.

Zig Ziglar once said, "You are what you are and you are where you are because of what has gone into your mind. You change what you are and you change where you are by changing what goes into your mind." Since I made that choice to change the people I hung around with and, in turn, make the choice to be with positive friends, I was able to start building up my better self-image. Had I continued to be in the midst of the wrong people, listen to unhealthy popular music, or read negative books, my self-image would have continued on its' downward spiral. Finding spiritually healthy friends, hearing uplifting and grace inspired songs, and reading the Bible enabled me to grow into who I am today and what I will become tomorrow.

Back in the early '80s, when the personal computer was coming of age, one of the popular sayings was, "garbage in, garbage out." What you entered into the memory of the computer was critical—if it was nonsense going in, you can be assured it would be nonsense coming out as well. It's the same with our lives. What books are we reading? What movies are we watching? What kinds of friends are we associating with?

Everything matters, and everything counts. Whatever you feed on is what will come out of you. Make sure you are feeding on the healthy stuff, and the results of healthy choices will be a vibrant and healthy life.

Now back to baseball. The baseball season went very well for us. We grew as a team as well as in our friendships with each other. As a team we had many successes, many opportunities for learning and growth. As our senior year baseball season came to a close, we had the awards banquet where some team members were honored for their performance. The team members themselves were those who cast ballots for many categories, including Most Valuable Player, highest batting average, and the leader in home runs. Much to my surprise, I was awarded the "Most Improved Player" trophy. There is no doubt that this award meant the world to me. It was an honor that people took note of the changes that I was making in my life, even though slow and gradual, they were acknowledged.

I was even more convinced that if I continued to apply the Ziglar principles, and the "Strategy" course concepts, the trajectory of my life would be changed forever. It was even apparent to my family members, my Mom and Dad, sisters and brother, that my confidence level was improved, I was more positive, and there was an excitement in my life. The change was happening slowly, but it was happening. I was overjoyed by the improvements on the ball field and with the relationships with others in my life.

I graduated from Saugus High School in 1980 at the age of 17. Many of my classmates were already 18, and at the time back then, I hadn't realized that I was competing with others who were nearly a year older than I was. At that age, one year can make a significant difference on performance within that peer group.

As I entered my college years, and my adult life, I knew I would be facing many more challenges, but now I felt I was better equipped with the tools I needed to march forward toward success. I continued to apply the Zig Ziglar principles to my life, but over time, my exposure to Zig Ziglar's messages faded. One particularly profound statement from Mr. Ziglar remains clear. "People often say that motivation doesn't last. Well, neither does bathing, that's why we recommend it daily."
Now we step into a time warp and fast forward my life to today. I graduated from College of the Canyons with an A.S. degree, and graduated from LIFE Pacific College with a B.A. degree. I have been married to my loving, supportive, wonderful wife, Melissa, for 15 years, and have two fabulous children, Anna and Joshua. Two dogs and one cat round out our household.

I have the same choices to make these days as I always did. I know that the input I allow into my mind and who I choose to hang around with will affect who I am. I will continue to choose wisely.

My top eight heroes of all time make up my short list. Jesus, Zig Ziglar, John Wooden, John Maxwell, Dave Ramsey, Pastor Jack Hayford, my Dad, Bob, and my Mom, Shirley.

I find that Zig Ziglar reminds me how valuable "Automobile University" is. I have taken that to heart. I am constantly listening to audio books in the car, or on my phone, or on my computer. My wife Melissa, and my best friend Curtis, can surely attest to that.

In addition, a quote from Charlie "Tremendous" Jones has had a big impact on me as well. "You will be the same person in five years as you are today except for the people you meet and the books you read." This has helped me seek out new friends and read (or listen to) new books. I am now on a quest to renew and rebuild myself. I feel like I'm in high school again. I am finding so many new ideas from the books I am reading and the new people I am meeting. It is awesome.

A few years ago, I found myself feeling alone and isolated, not really knowing what to do with the swimming pool service and repair business I had started. In addition, I was not managing my money well. Melissa, my wife, asked me what I wanted for Christmas that year, and I replied, "Well, I really don't know, but how about an audio book about business or money, or something like that."

This insightful and caring wife of mine delivered. In my Christmas stocking that early morning, I found a book called "The Total Money Make Over" by Dave Ramsey. It was great – the downside was that I did not listen to it until April of the next year. It just sat, unopened, in my truck. I had not a clue who Dave Ramsey was or what he was teaching.

Now, after opening it up, plugging it in and listening to it nine times in a row—no joke—I now had a financial game plan drilled into my mind that would lead me down a road to prosperity and financial certainty. Something about that bit of "what goes in...comes out!"

While listening to some of Dave Ramsey's radio broadcasts, I learned that he belonged to a men's group that met once a week in his office. It was called the "Eagles Group." Dave met with these men to endorse accountability, personal growth, and moral support. This discovery led me to think that I could use a similar tactic. I looked around and found a group at my church, already in place, called Men@Work. It was made up of 10-15 businessmen who met weekly for the same focus points that Dave Ramsey's group did. A gentleman named Rob Izer led the group and I, personally, found continued growth occurring inside me by my attendance every week.

The format was simple. We would watch a DVD or online instruction for 30 minutes and then have a discussion on that topic for the next 30 minutes. We would challenge each other to grow and learn from each of those studies.

Over the course of the study sessions, our leader, Rob, was called to another ministry and left our group. The existing group members then selected me to lead the group, and I was humbled and, at the same time challenged, to step up and take over the group. Following the guidelines of author John Maxwell, "Personal growth does not happen automatically, it has to be intentional," I took the position, and my new goal was to become a servant leader like the example Jesus gave us.

Being a part of this group reinvigorated me to refresh my familiarity with the Zig Ziglar materials. I began to listen, again, to the materials online and in print, fueling my desires to lead with sound practices. In one online visit, I noted that Zig Ziglar's son, Tom, had a Facebook account. I made that contact, and further learned that he would be in Phoenix, Arizona, holding a seminar with another business trainer (Howard Partridge) at an upcoming date. I attended that conference and met both men, further motivating myself to continue my personal growth.

While pursuing my work in business and leadership, I learned of the new "Ziglar Legacy Certified Training Course" offered by the Ziglar Company. I signed up for the course, and embarked on this new pathway. I was confident in my ability to embrace the three powerful components of this course. My "Personal Development", my ability to "Build Winning Relationships", and my dedication to "Goal Setting and Achievement."

Now that I have completed and graduated from this training, I am on a quest to add value to people's lives in any way I can. This chapter in this book is one of the steps I'm taking to get myself out of my "comfort zone" and grow myself. I'm the last one of all the authors in this book to turn my chapter in, largely due to my procrastination. I am going to get this done, and now I'm almost there.

Jesus has forgiven me and set me free from the bondage of sin. Zig Ziglar has helped me develop a positive self image of myself, helped me with understanding how important it is to live a balanced life using the seven parts of the Ziglar Wheel of Life as my guide. They show me how to develop a goals program to operate by, as well as how valuable automobile university is and I have taken that to heart.

John Wooden has given me the two sets of three *Never Lie, Never Cheat, Never Steal,* and *Don't whine, Don't Complain and Don't Make Excuses.* Also, the Seven point creed:

1. Be true to yourself
2. Make each day your masterpiece.
3. Help others.
4. Drink deeply from good books, especially the Bible.
5. Make friendship a fine art.
6. Build a shelter against a rainy day.

7. Pray for guidance and give thanks for your blessings every day.

I learned from John Maxwell that personal growth is not automatic, it has to be intentional. Dave Ramsey taught me how to get out of debt, stay out of debt, build wealth and create a legacy for future generations. Pastor Jack taught me how to pray, the importance of the Bible and how to listen to the Holy Spirits guidance in my life. My Dad taught me how to make Jesus number one in my life more than anything else and my Mom taught me how to be a giver and how to be sensitive to others.

One of the significant reasons that I am writing a chapter for this Ziglar book came from the encouragement of one member of my 'Men@Work' business group. Shawn Gorham, gave me $20.00 seed money to help me write my first book. I want to include him in this chapter since this is the first book to which I have contributed. I'm hoping to write my first full book in the future. With encouragement and support from friends like Shawn, I know my dream can become a reality. I also want to acknowledge a few of the other guys from the Men@Work group, which I always said was my best meeting of the week. Thank you, John Waters, Jim Ritterhouse, Paul Pastore, Bob Doyle, Steve Weber, and Thor Thomsen (who is now doing a great job as the new leader). These guys have encouraged me to grow, develop, get into better physical condition, become closer to Jesus, become a better business owner, a better husband, dad, and overall leader. Thank you, guys.

These guys have also challenged me to become a part of Toastmasters International. Zig Ziglar always recommended this great organization, and I have learned a great deal from joining the Dobson Ranch Toastmasters Club #4705. Zig Ziglar always said, "You can't take the elevator to success, you always have to take the stairs."

The way to achieve a balanced, successful life, to acquire Health, Wealth, Happiness, Friends, Growth, Peace, Security Leisure, Freedom, Opportunity, is to take the first step of developing a healthy self-image.

The next step is to build winning relationships with others. Then create a goals program that can get you where you want to go.

The next step is to have the right attitude. Zig Ziglar always said, "Your attitude, not your aptitude, will determine your altitude."

And the next step up the stairs is hard work; then it's your desire that will get you to the top of the stairs to reach success in life. The journey getting there is what life is all about. God wants us all to keep growing, learning, and teaching others what we have learned until the day we die.

So, you might ask, "What's so great about Zig Ziglar?" In short, when you expose yourself to Mr. Ziglar's powerful, positive messages and principles, you can change your life for the better if you apply these principles to your life. The big word here is "IF." Take action. Don't wait for something to happen. Make something happen.

Zig Ziglar introduced me to a new way of thinking about myself, about my life, and what I could accomplish with my life. It all started with my self-image. Once I changed the way I thought about myself, I would be able to accomplish whatever I set out to do. No more dead ends for my life.

Zig Ziglar said that one of the greatest of all of the emotions in life is to have an attitude of gratitude. Therefore, this last group of guys I want to thank for having a big supportive impact in my life is the guys who were in my wedding. I want to thank Bob Penberthy, Don Salladin, Jerrod Sessler, Nathan Heatherly and last but not least John Kouri. Thanks guys for all of your love, advice and encouragement over the years. You all have impacted me in a profound way.

I believe God has a plan for all of our lives, even though we all do the best we can to mess up the plan God has for us. God sees past our shortcomings. We need to see ourselves the way God sees us. Then, and only then, will we be able to live in the fullness of joy He promises us. If I had never attended Saugus High School, I never would have met the Coach who taught the Class and introduced me to the Book which helped me learn the principles of the Man (Zig Ziglar) who changed the Trajectory of My Life. May Jesus bless you in a great way for reading this book and this chapter of the book. I hope my story and my words have helped you in some way

I end with this Bible verse that is more powerful to me today than ever before in my life: "3 Why do you look at the speck of sawdust in your brother's eye and pay no attention to the plank in your own eye? 4 How can you say to your brother, 'Let me take the speck out of your eye,' when all the time there is a plank in your own eye? 5 You hypocrite, first take the plank out of your own eye, and then you will see clearly to remove the speck from your brother's eye." (Matthew 7:3-5, New International Version (NIV) We all need to look at ourselves in the mirror first and straighten out the mess you see there before you try to go out and straighten out the people you have in your life. And I'm not sure who came up with this, but I love this quote I saw on one of my friends' Facebook page: "Who are you going to blame your life on today?" Wow, that is a powerful question to ask yourself daily. You are never going to change anybody else until you change you first. ✑

RICK R RICHARDS

Rick R Richards (www.RickRRichards.com) is proud to be a Zig Ziglar Legacy Certified Trainer. It is a dream come true for him. When the opportunity arose to become certified, Rick jumped on it. He signed up and was accepted to be part of the first certified class. He bought his airplane tickets and paid for his hotel stay in advance. However, due to personal conflicts and his wife tearing the ACL in her left knee and injuring her MCL and meniscus a few days before the training, he had to postpone his certification until the second training. Rick is excited and honored to teach the Ziglar message to young and old who have never heard it. There are masses of people who desperately need to understand the principles Ziglar, Inc., stands for and lives by.

Rick is the Founder/CEO of Arizona Quality Pool Service & Repair, LLC, (www.azqpools.net) located in Gilbert, Arizona. They have been in business since 2004. The company helps people maintain and repair their swimming pools in and around the east valley of Phoenix where there is no shortage of pools to maintain or repair. The company's motto is "We CARE, Clean and Repair." The emphasis is on the CARE part and going the extra mile.

Before Rick started his own service-based business, he worked in corporate America in information technology sales. He worked for Avnet, Inc., (www.avnet.com) and Insight (www.insight.com) selling hardware and software for almost six years. Rick is a graduate of LIFE Pacific College (www.lifepacific.edu) located in San Dimas, California. He earned his B.A. in Pastoral Ministries and was ordained as a minister with the International Church of the Foursquare Gospel (www.foursquare.org). Reverend Richard Robert Richards is a long title—the fact that his new title has four R's in it causes many discussions about how he acquired such a unique name. Ask him how his parents came up with his name sometime—it's an interesting conversation. Rick worked at a number of churches over the years and served in a variety of ministry positions, including janitor, photographer, and youth pastor.

Rick is in the process of writing his first full-length book entitled 1% Change (www.1percentchange.com). It is scheduled for release in the Fall of 2015. Rick believes that, when many people look at themselves in the mirror and honestly assess where they are at in life, they can become discouraged and overwhelmed. This book is designed to bring hope to people who feel they can never make something of themselves. It's all about making small, manageable, one-percent changes day by day which will bring great progress in time. Great change happens slowly if you are committed to the process; this book will help people who feel stuck and motivate them to remain committed to change and growth little by little, day by day.

Rick is a member of Toastmasters International and is excited to realize all the personal and leadership growth he has achieved by being involved in this great organization. Rick loves to coordinate Dave Ramsey Financial Peace University (FPU) classes and the Legacy Journey classes. If you, a friend, or a family member need help managing your personal finances, you can find great help at www.daveramsey.com where you can find a local class to attend, listen to Dave teach, or find wonderfully helpful resources.

Rick is also embarking on a new concept of personal growth called The Strategy Club (www.thestrategy.club), of which he is the Founder/CEO. The club's concept is connected to the "Wheel of Life" principles Zig Ziglar teaches on becoming successful in life by being balanced and strong in ALL areas of life, not just a few. This club encourages its members to become healthy physically, financially, emotionally, and spiritually through its fitness classes, nutrition seminars, *financial training, emotional counseling, and spiritual guidance—all while using the Bible as one's road map to life.*

You can contact Rick R Richards at:

2733 E. Majestic Eagle
Gilbert, AZ 85297
480-695-POOL (7665)
azqpools.net@gmail.com
www.azqpools.net
Rick@RickRRichards.com
www.RickRRichards.com
www.thestrategy.club
www.1percentchange.com
www.ziglarcertified.com/Sites/Index.asp?PIN=41605&SN=RickRich-
ards&IVID=0

THE EXCELLENCE EFFECT

———————

By Justin Young

If success is your desired destination, then excellence is the vehicle that
will take you there. — J. Justin Young

EXCELLENCE IS DEFINED as the quality of being outstanding or extremely good. Its Latin root, excellere, means "to surpass." I believe that
deep within all of us lies the desire for excellence, the desire to be an
outstanding individual who is extremely good at what he or she does—
an individual of high moral character, of good reputation, a shining
example to our family and community. We do not just want to be good;
we want to be better than good, surpassing every limitation. Excellence
is not mystical; there is no magic formula. Excellence is achieved by
what we do or do not do on a daily basis. Excellence is a decision.
Aristotle said it like this: "We are what we repeatedly do. Therefore
excellence is not an act but a habit."

I believe that excellence honors God and inspires people. At the
moment that you begin to do the very best with what you've been giv-
en, at that moment, excellence will begin to affect every area of your
life, bringing a profound effect on the quality of your life. The great

American football coach, Vince Lombardi, said that, "The quality of a person's life is in direct proportion to his or her commitment to excellence, regardless of his or her field of endeavor." As people are inspired by your example and the spirit of excellence that you embody, a power is released that brings key relationships into place. Excellence brings in multiplication where previously only simple addition had existed. What I am describing will help you be, do, and have more in life. What I am describing is called "The Excellence Effect."

The desire to excel in our field of endeavor, our relationships, our finances, and every aspect of life is ingrained deep within our DNA. The truth is that no child grows up wanting to live a life of mediocrity or lack. As children we wake up with excitement, the world holds opportunity, and we can't wait to grow up and BE something! How often do you hear children telling everyone what they want to be when they grow up? I have three children at home, and I can tell you that they are sincerely optimistic; they're excited about what the future holds. Zig Ziglar said it like this: "Man was designed for accomplishment, engineered for success, and endowed with seeds of greatness."

So if we all are born with the seeds of greatness inside us, if it is in our DNA as human beings to live a life of accomplishment and success, what happens to so many people? Why do they seem to be just surviving, simply dragging their way through life? Let me tell you from experience that life has a way of beating you down if you let it. Somewhere between school ending and adulthood beginning many people begin to become disengaged and disillusioned. Reality begins to hit and what our parents always referred to as "the real world" begins to become real on a whole new level.

We find that things don't just fall in our lap, but that we are going to have to begin to put in effort like never before, work extremely hard, and sometimes even fight when necessary. Often times, after years of working, trying, fighting for our dreams, goals, and visions, we become weary. Complacency sets in, and we just give up. We keep working, we do what we need to do to survive, but we surrender to a mundane existence. We settle for a life of mediocrity and believe the lie that all we will ever be is average. Can I tell you that you were not created to merely survive. You were created to thrive! You were created to live a life of excellence!

Excellence vs. Perfection

I've found that many times people shut down and turn off their receptors the moment they hear the word "Excellence," especially when it's spoken in terms of a core value to be put into practice for their daily life. It's almost as if you just slid a giant mountain in front of them and yelled, "Now climb!" The very thought of tackling that mountain is so daunting that they throw their hands up and say, "What's the use?" They simply give up. The challenge seems too big, the mission too consuming. I sincerely believe after a decade of working with people that it's not that most people are lazy, or intentionally belligerent when it comes to living in excellence, it's that they think Excellence is something else altogether! It's a case of mistaken identity.

Excellence has an impostor—it's called "Perfection." The greatest enemy of excellence will always be perceived perfection. Let me say clearly that perfection has nothing to do with excellence. And let me parenthetically inject that neither does success. Let's call perfection what it is—an Illusion! It's not real, it doesn't exist. Perfection is the hallucination of a dangling carrot leading individuals down a twisted, tiring rabbit trail with no destination in sight. It will rob you of peace, joy, and love, leaving you broke, busted, and disgusted in the end. Chasing perfection will leave you with a life of regret. Pursuit of what we perceive to be perfection leaves a wake of loss in our life—loss of time, relationships, finances, and authentic opportunities.

So I get it. Just talking about it is exhausting. But don't give up on excellence just because of what someone told you it would require. In a world where something better is always marketed to us in a way to make us dissatisfied with what we currently have or the way we may look, it's sometimes hard to keep our focus. Don't drink the Kool-Aid. The pursuit of perfection will kill your God-given passion. The practice of excellence fuels those God-given passions and empowers your dreams, your visions, and your goals.

Understanding the Excellence Effect

To fully understand the Excellence Effect we must first have a complete understanding of the terms associated with this concept. One of the most commonly mistaken grammatical errors is the usage of "Affect versus Effect." I'll be the first to admit that I have struggled with this one myself from time to time. Affect, with an "a," means "to influence." An example of usage would be: "The cold weather has affected my body temperature." Affect is most commonly used as a verb. Effect, with an "e," is usually a noun with many subtle meanings, however at their core you will always find that effect is "a result." An example of usage here would be: "The cold temperatures had no effect on me," or "The sound effects were awesome." Lastly, we use the term "infect." When we think of this term we automatically think about sickness or disease. We immediately associate it with some aspect of the human body or medical field. Although at its root infect simply means "to invade, penetrate, and permeate." Affect, Effect and Infect are the key components in a quote I use that represents the core process by which the Excellence Effect takes place in my life and yours.

> The Affect of Excellence will always produce the Effect of Excellence and the effect of excellence will Infect every aspect of your life.
> — J. Justin Young

Excellence really is contagious! It catches on and has a dramatically positive effect on life. When my wife and I had our first child it brought so much in my life full circle. I saw things in a much greater depth than I had previously. I now saw the world through the eyes of a father! I instantly realized that there were so many layers to life that I had not previously known. Granted, they had been there all along, but I was unaware. Like many, I thought I knew how I would feel as a father. I would listen to parents talk so descriptively about how different they instantly felt and how the world changed. I knew, obviously, that much responsibility would come, and that life would change as it pertained to schedules, demands, and amounts of sleep, but I never realized the weightiness of what they were explaining. I will never forget the moment that our daughter was delivered and I heard her first cry. I felt like Neo in the sci-fi action movie "The Matrix." I felt as if I had just been connected to a whole new world, a world much more alive, more vibrant, and with a now greater purpose than I had previously known.

Now, several years later, I have come to realize the beautiful effect that a newborn child has. The child affects not just the parents, but everyone the child touches—grandparents, aunts, uncles, cousins, family friends, church congregations. Everything changes; there's no going back! The covenant of love between my wife and me had affected us. The affect made possible for a moment of conception. That conception took us through a process that gave us another effect as our precious daughter was born, and the effect of that birth instantly and supernaturally infected our entire family and many friends with a new depth and quality of life and love that we had not formerly known.

Excellence in the same way will affect, effect, and infect every area of your life if you are committed to it. You must first make a covenant with yourself to practice excellence. It must become a daily habit that you pick up and put on as you would your tie or your shoes. You don't have to pursue it. You need not chase after it. You have it already. You must simply practice it. Excellence is developed by persistent consistency. Doing the small things daily will give you big results over time. If you are consistently faithful with the small things, eventually you will be given much.

You were placed on this earth with everything you need. You were equipped before the foundation of the world. It may come as a surprise to you, but every tool you need is already on board. Excellence is resident in you.

Get a Vision

To begin to operate in Excellence you must first get a vision for what excellence in your life will look like. It is paramount that you understand that vision will always empower your mission. We have a great ability, the ability to be able to see something before it ever physically manifests. I call this faith.

Faith is the substance of things hoped for and evidence of things not yet seen. Faith is the power that enables visionary leaders like you and I to be able to look out and see what can be in areas that may seem barren to the natural eye. It is going to take faith to carry out your vision. There will be difficult times as you move forward, times of hardship, times of doubt. It will not be easy but it will be worth your effort.

I love how novelist E.L. Doctorow describes having vision in a difficult time—what I often refer to as a "night season." "It's like driving a car at night. You never see farther than your headlights, but you can make the whole trip that way." Sometimes, life clouds our vision and we cannot see clearly or see as far perhaps as we previously could, but as Zig Ziglar said, "When you begin moving towards your goals, just travel as far as you can see, and once you get there you'll be able to see even further."

I spell the word faith, R-I-S-K. Faith will always require an element of risk. It is imperative that you buy into your vision, that you yourself are all in, 100 percent sold, so that as you take a risk and step out in faith towards excellence, difficulty and negativity will not be able to detour you. The only failure in life is the person who fails to get up after falling. A vision is much more than seeing. It is believing; it is an experience. The great thing about a person with an experience is that they are never at the mercy of a person with an opinion.

One of my favorite books is a book called Leadership Excellence, written by Pat Williams. Among the many stories about great leaders highlighted in this book, a particular story about Walt Disney resonates with me and gives what I believe is a stellar example of moving in faith toward your vision.

In the 1950s Walt Disney began to meet with teams of architects, engineers, and contractors as preparations were being made to begin construction on Disneyland. It was a huge undertaking and much planning would be required before beginning construction of the new theme park. As the initial plans were laid out, the team of professionals assembled all agreed that it would be wise to begin with the outer areas of the park and work their way inward. This would enable them to use roads, water, and all existing infrastructure as they worked their way in to the center of the park.

The center of the park is where the princess's castle was going to be, and working from the outside inward would save a tremendous amount of time and financial resources. While this made sense from the standpoint of conventional wisdom, Walt did not agree. He proceeded to explain to his team that they would approach the construction in reverse, building the princess's castle first and then working their way outward. You see, Walt Disney wanted that castle to tower over the park grounds so that every day as workers arrived they would see the excellence of what they were building. He wanted them to be able to catch his vision and be inspired to carry out the rest of the park with the same excellence. While this made no sense to some, it made perfect sense to Walt Disney, because he was the visionary.

Walt saw Disneyland long before anyone else. That castle that was once just a dream and a vision is now one of the most recognizable brands in the world—an international symbol of excellence, of what is now a multi billion-dollar company that has brought joy and changed the lives of countless children all over the world.

Your vision, or how you approach your vision, may not always make sense to everyone. Walt Disney's certainly didn't. But trust your heart. You may have to contradict popular opinion or what conventional wisdom may tell you, but don't allow contrary opinions, negativity, or current lack to keep you from moving forward. Keep trusted advisors close and guard your vision from adversaries. Begin today moving in excellence.

Get Rid of Negativity

In order to live a life of excellence you must remove the negativity. Negativity clouds your focus and will eventually wear you down. Raise the rent on negativity and kick it out of your life. There are two main highways that negativity uses to access our lives: It comes either through our own "stink'n think'n" or through relationships.

We must first win the battle between our own two ears and eliminate any negative thought cycles. We must learn to develop a positive self-image by learning from our defeats, focusing on our victories, and moving forward. There will always be negativity in life, but it does not have to abide in you. Your focus is extremely important. What you focus on, you empower. Do not magnify and empower negativity by giving it your attention. Learn to focus on the positive and verbalize those things through positive self-talk.

There is power in the tongue. What you speak is extremely important. You cannot live a life of excellence if you are constantly concentrating on and verbalizing defeat. The word in your mouth will always become a work in your hand. Your words can develop into a positive or negative work depending on what you speak. I love what the Bible says in James 3:4 where we read: "Or take ships as an example. Although they are so large and are driven by strong winds, they are steered by a very small rudder wherever the pilot wants to go." Our tongue is a small muscle, but it can control our entire life.

If you think and speak defeat and despair, you will live defeat and despair. Likewise, if you think and speak positivity and prosperity, you will reap those benefits. So just remember, words are like seeds being planted in the ground—they will produce a harvest.

Negativity also comes through other people. Everyone knows someone who always seems to have something negative to say, someone who is critical and judgmental of everything and everybody. Always remember that people too weak to follow through on their own vision and goal will always find a way to criticize and discourage yours. Zig Ziglar put it this way: "The only taste of success that some people ever get is when they take a bite out of you."

Some people need drama like they need oxygen. Do not tolerate the company of people who have constant chaos in their life. While there are exceptions, most people with chaotic lives are not simply victims of uncontrollable circumstances. The chaos dwells in them. In life we have to deal with enough negativity without inviting it in on ourselves, so know your circle! Make absolutely sure that everyone in your boat is holding a paddle and not a drill. Oftentimes, some of the very people who we think are there to help us paddle are actually trying to sink us.

Other times, some of the people closest to us may mean well, but they may have a negative opinion or outlook of our vision and goal. In those cases we have to adjust our filter. You have to have the discernment and courage to be able to listen, but also to know when you need to continue to move forward.

Get Moving

It's been said that the greatest day in a person's life is not the day they are born, but the day they find out why. Once you get a vision, and you begin to move in excellence toward your vision, and you have removed the negativity, then it is time to get moving! Start today. Never look back, and never give up. There will be obstacles thrown in your path along the way, but always remember that forward movement turns obstacles into opportunities. Too many people give up, not realizing that they are on the cusp of breakthrough. Often when the battle is strongest, the victory is closest. George Barna said, "Vision without perseverance is like an interesting chapter in an unfinished book." We must persist in our purpose.

We persist by eliminating doubt. A double-minded man is unstable in all his ways. You must pick a horse and ride it. You cannot do everything, and you cannot be all things to all people. Find what you are good at and make it excellent! I have witnessed so many people in life who constantly waiver in their opinions. They can't seem to make a decision and stick to it to save their life. Relationally, spiritually, vocationally, they are all over the map.

You can spend your life trying to be a jack of all trades and know a little about a lot but it will not get you very far. You will end up so stretched out and overextended that you are no good to anyone. When you don't pick an area of focus, you end up frustrated and burnt out before you even get started, straining relationships and your home life. You cannot build anything of lasting significance in life without a team. No man is an island to himself, and an unpredictable leader will produce tentative followers. Excellence requires stability, persistency and consistency.

The Excellence Effect in Everyday Life

I want to end by telling you a story about my life, a story that I believe brings the message of the Excellence Effect full circle. I come from a great family. My siblings and I grew up in a loving home with great parents, and we were raised wonderfully. We were not wealthy, but my parents worked hard to provide for us to the very best of their ability, often making large sacrifices for our financial well-being and happiness.

It was the late '80s and my parents had finally arrived at a place where they were able to build our family's first home. They bought two acres of land out in the country and built a 1,400-square-foot home. That two-acre plot of land was next to a fence that enclosed a farm pasture that bordered our property. After living there a while, I came to befriend a horse that stayed in that pasture. I loved animals and had a particular affection towards horses. After living in the city in a small apartment it had become a dream of my family to one day have our own farm animals, particularly a horse.

The thing about the late '80s is that it was a tough financial climate. Interest was high and for a middle-class family we were just happy to be out of the city and able to purchase the land and build the home. Too young to understand, I didn't quite realize at my young age what a massive investment an animal of that size was. I didn't understand that you couldn't just buy a horse and that would be the end of it, that they ate tremendous amounts of food, needed a lot of fence and a barn, among many other things. My parents were wise and didn't go into debt to gratify an immediate want but they kept the dream alive and encouraged us kids to as well.

I came to learn that the horse next door had a name, Vandel, and Vandel was not just any horse. He was a quarter horse, and not just any quarter horse, but a direct descendant of a famous bloodline for that breed. He was beautiful; he was bay in color with four white stockings and a white star in the center of his forehead. I would come home from school in the afternoon and take a carrot or an apple or whatever I could nab from the kitchen and head out to the fence to talk to Vandel and share an afternoon snack. We became buddies, and even though I knew we could never afford a horse like Vandel, I had a vision to one day be able to own and ride one just like him.

After some time had passed, one Saturday morning my dad woke me up and told me to get ready, that we were going to the hardware store. At the hardware store I watched as several men loaded bags of concrete mix and several posts into the back of the truck. On the ride home I questioned my dad about what the project for the day was going to be, and he told me that we were going home to begin work on a fence. You cannot imagine the excitement! As kids often do I expected we would build the fence on Saturday and have a horse by Sunday. Of course, that was not the case.

The funds were still not there for a horse but my dad made a decision that morning: He decided that, even though we couldn't write a check, blink our eyes, and do it all at once, we were going to step out. He decided that, even though we may not have a lot and we may not be able to do it all immediately, we could start—we could begin. We were only able to buy a few posts that day but we bought what we could afford. We went home and my dad took a pair of post hole diggers and began digging the holes for the fence posts we had purchased, and by the end of that Saturday we had a great start to a long-held family dream and vision.

Every Saturday from then forward we would buy as many posts as we could afford, some weeks we bought a lot and some weeks we bought a few, but we never gave up. We did the very best with what we had! We had decided that we could sit around and wait forever for circumstances and finances to get "just right," or we could begin with what we had, go as far as we could see that Saturday, and then plan and prepare for the next week. Every weekend we would accomplish more and more.

Not long after starting the fence project we were given a saddle and a rope. My dad would fasten the saddle to the few sections of fence that were finished and my brother and I would put on our western shirt, boots and cowboy hat and sit on that saddle for hours, pretending that it was our horse. I am sure that we looked a little off-center to a lot people as they drove by our property and saw us spurring a fence and yelling "giddy up," but we didn't care—we were speaking our dream.

An awesome thing happened in our lives as we began to work hard and, with persistence, consistently move toward our dream. People began to take notice. Friends of my parents would ride by and see the work, stop, and ask what we were building—and some began to get out and help. This grew over time until on Saturdays more and more people were showing up—people who were skilled in construction, people who had the tools to do the job more efficiently. We no longer had to dig holes by hand because a man lent us his tractor with a large auger bit. We no longer had to hammer nails by hand because a friend brought an air-compressed nail gun.

Before we knew it, the fence project was complete and we moved right into building a barn. We had ten or twelve people showing up most Saturdays. My mother would cook large lunches to feed everyone as they worked. It was an exciting time. Hardware store owners were hearing about the project through some of the workers and would donate windows and doors that they had at their store. It was amazing! In just a few short months not only did we have a fence but we had a nice barn with four horse stalls, a tack and feed room, and a hay loft! To just ride by you would have thought we were real-life ranchers!

Shortly after the barn was built, I came home from school one day and my parents told me that the day had come! We were finally getting a horse, as a matter of fact we already had the horse! I ran through the door across the backyard and jumped the fence, made a sharp right turn into the alleyway of the barn and there the horse stood! It was magnificent! Bay in color—just like I wanted—four white stockings, and a white star in the center of his forehead, and then it hit me. This horse looked very familiar. It was Vandel! I couldn't believe it. By this time my parents had rounded the corner with big smiles on their faces. They explained that the neighbor had made Vandel available to us at a great price that they were able to afford. I was ecstatic! Not only did we now have a horse, but we had the very one that I had spent every afternoon with, never thinking we would ever be able to own.

After purchasing Vandel we were given another horse as a gift, so now my dad had a horse of his own and we were able to ride together. We later purchased another, and another, which led to buying more property and building a bigger barn, until eventually we had 50 acres, 12 horses, and kept an average of 60 head of cattle. Many of the men who worked on the fence and barn project with us also bought horses, and we would all take weekend trips riding. We had a tremendous amount of fun during those years.

Living this story as an adolescent taught me a lot about life. You and I have to take a step. We have to begin to move on our dreams and visions. We can either take a step forward or sit around forever and complain about the resources, training, or knowledge that we don't have. When my parents made the decision to begin to do the very best with what they had, things began to happen for us. We did not have all the pieces, we simply stepped out in faith and began to consistently persist in our purpose.

You may feel as if the vision for your life is a million miles away, but let me encourage you today that it is closer than you think—it is in your reach! I didn't know if we would ever be able to afford a nice horse, but little did I know that every day when I walked over to the fence bordering our property, I was petting my horse all along. It seemed a million miles away even though it had actually been placed right next door for me. The vision was there, it was simply waiting on us to make a move.

Many people never get to own their horse, live their dream, or walk in their vision because they never plan and prepare. In the same way that you can't own a horse without somewhere to put him, you can't live your dream without first doing the practical things and building the structure to house it. Many people who want to have the providential have never done the practical. Begin working on you, become a student; learn, grow, build your character; take a step, and begin to use and do the very best with what you have, and more will come.

As we took a step and began to work on the fence each week using what we had, it began to inspire people. We may have only been able to afford four posts to bury some weeks, but we made sure they were placed properly, that they were level, and that we had done an excellent job. This inspired people and released the power of synergy as friends and family began to catch the vision and join alongside us bringing resources with them and increasing our efficiency.

We were being fulfilled as they helped us get what we wanted in life, and they were fulfilled because they were able to function in their gifting. Together we were able to accomplish so much more; new relationships were gained and old relationships were strengthened. Through those relationships more resources were released than we ever could have imagined. This inspiration moved through the whole group as many of these people purchased horses themselves. Excellence really is contagious! Zig Ziglar's core message is: "You can have everything you want in life if you'll just help enough other people get what they want."

Always remember: Excellence honors God and inspires people. Live and demonstrate a life of excellence by using what you have, where you are, to the very best of your ability—and watch things begin to accelerate for you. You have to start somewhere. You may not have a lot, but make sure that you do the best with what you have and watch it multiply and become more. Persist in your purpose and you will experience a life lived in excellence. ✎

JUSTIN YOUNG

Justin Young is a motivational speaker, business consultant, and trainer. He is certified and endorsed by The Ziglar Corporation (Zig Ziglar Legacy Certification) and travels the United States and abroad as a keynote for corporate conventions, municipalities, social organizations, churches, and nonprofits. Delivering a core message of excellence and its profound effect on every aspect of life, Justin also teaches Zig Ziglar's proven workshops on topics such as "Building the Best You," "Building Winning Relationships" and "Goal Setting and Achievement." An aspiring author, his first book, The Excellence Effect, *is set for release in early 2015. Justin's life mission is to "Impact, Impart, and Empower Leaders to Experience a Life Lived in Excellence."*

www.jjustinyoung.com
justin@excellence-effect.com
1-844-JJY-Excellence

CPSIA information can be obtained at www.ICGtesting.com
Printed in the USA
LVOW04s1245281114

415908LV00008B/30/P